The ALCHEM`

6 Essential Shifts
in Mindsets and Habits
to Achieve World Peace

The ALCHEMY *of* PEACE

6 Essential Shifts
in Mindsets and Habits
to Achieve World Peace

Sovaida Ma'ani Ewing

CPGG | CENTER FOR PEACE & GLOBAL GOVERNANCE
Principled Solutions to Global Problems

THE ALCHEMY OF PEACE: 6 ESSENTIAL SHIFTS IN MINDSETS AND HABITS TO ACHIEVE WORLD PEACE

Copyright © 2020 by Sovaida Ma'ani Ewing. All rights reserved. Except for brief quotations in a review, this book, or parts thereof, must not be reproduced in any form without permission in writing from the publisher. For information, address Center for Peace and Global Governance at sovaidamaani@cpgg.org.

Center for Peace and Global Governance <cpgg.org>

Designed by Kenneth P. Ewing

ISBN 978-1-7331578-1-0 (paper)

ISBN 978-1-7331578-2-7 (electronic)

Cataloging information:

Author: Sovaida Ma'ani Ewing

Title: The Alchemy Of Peace: 6 Essential Shifts in Mindsets and Habits to Achieve World Peace

Subjects: peace—psychological aspects; international security; peace studies; peace—prerequisites; leadership; leadership—character; leadership—psychological aspects; leadership—corruption; political science—mindsets and habits; political science—globalization; political science—nationalism; political science—international institutions; political science—global ethics; motivation (psychological aspects)

For information about bulk purchases, please email sovaidamaani@cpgg.org or write to us at

Center for Peace and Global Governance
Sales Department
4201 Cathedral Ave NW Suite 715E
Washington, DC 20016

To Ken, Gigi, and Baharieh, who accept me as I am and unfailingly shower me with the gift of their unwavering love and support

The ALCHEMY *of* PEACE

6 Essential Shifts
in Mindsets and Habits
to Achieve World Peace

Contents

"Be anxiously concerned with the needs of the age ye live in and center your deliberations on its exigencies and requirements."

BAHA'U'LLAH[1]

"What is the use of living, if it be not to strive for noble causes and to make this muddled world a better place for those who will live in it after we are gone?... Humanity will not be cast down. We are going on swinging bravely forward along the grand high road and already behind the distant mountains is the promise of the sun."

WINSTON CHURCHILL[2]

Introduction

We live at a critical time in the history of our evolution as a human race. It is an age of great upheaval and collective transition from humanity's adolescence to its maturity. Consequently, it is a time fraught with peril yet rich in promise. How we emerge from this period depends on how well we can summon our powers of imagination to envision who we, as a collective humanity, want to be going forward and what kind of world we want to live in. It also depends on how well we can identify the opportunities and gifts hidden within the contemporary calamities and how we choose to use them. If we fail to seize these opportunities, our collective human suffering will only grow deeper.

Right now, the global community finds itself increasingly buffeted by social, economic, environmental, and political forces it can neither fathom nor control. Between race, gender, and sex discrimination; environmental catastrophes; persistent economic disparities; and the disintegration of international peace and security, every corner of the globe is afflicted. Human beings everywhere are suffering. Whether physical, emotional, or psychological, humanity's anguish is unprecedentedly deep and universal. While there are many global challenges that threaten us, it is worth briefly contemplating three particular global crises that pose a dire threat to our lives.

The first is the world-encircling pandemic caused by the new coronavirus disease, COVID-19, which burst on the stage of international life at the end of 2019 and engulfed us in its grip in 2020. The pandemic has touched every corner of the earth, bringing physical suffering and mass deaths, which in turn have resulted in great emotional and mental suffering and engendered tremendous fear. In a desperate attempt to contain and mitigate its effects, nations have imposed quarantines and lock-downs of unprecedented scope on their populations. They have also severely restricted the movement of people and goods, interrupting human activity and patterns of behavior at all levels. People cannot venture out to work, visit friends, dine in restaurants, or move around freely without maintaining a safe social distance and arming themselves with masks and gloves. Sporting events, religious ceremonies, musical and artistic performances, and festivals have been canceled. Manufacturing and industry have been severely disrupted, with factories unable to receive the raw materials to create their goods and to ship their products out reliably. The price of oil and gas has dropped. Travel has been seriously curtailed; countries have closed their borders; supply chains have been interrupted; schools have moved their classes online; offices, workspaces, and businesses have shut their doors; houses of worship have closed; and governments have adjusted the way they conduct their work. Hospital staff are consistently endangered because of the woeful insufficiency of personal protective equipment required to keep health workers safe—a threat reflected in the number of workers who have caught the virus. Moreover, the pandemic is projected to bring a global recession the likes of which we have not seen since the Great Depression. The fear of recession is causing governments to ease lockdowns with unsafe haste in order to avert catastrophic economic consequences and starvation. Authorities are caught between a rock and a hard place; they find themselves having to choose between keeping their people safe from the virus on one hand and the threat of unsustainable unemployment and economic collapse on the other.

Yet, the damage caused by the COVID-19 virus is not limited to the physical and economic. The pandemic is also uncovering the gross ineptitude of our leaders and layers of institutional and cultural racism, xenophobia, and social and economic disparities—among other social ills—that have always been latent in our societies, but that have been aggravated in recent months.

When the coronavirus started to spread beyond China's borders in early 2020, fears about the transmission of the deadly virus fed into underlying prejudices, and instances of anti-Chinese racism and xenophobia started climbing. Chinese people were ostracized, verbally abused, and often told to return to their country. Their businesses slowed to a halt as people refused to buy from Chinese vendors. People of Asian descent—regardless of how long they had lived in Western countries, or if they were even of Chinese origin—became targets of racism and anger. While many of these prejudices have existed for decades, the coronavirus created an opportunity for the monster of xenophobia to rear its ugly head yet again.[3]

Meanwhile, another one of the most baneful social ills that we had swept under the rug also resurfaced. Anti-Black racism in the United States that had long been embedded in the nation's institutions, laws, and culture was forcibly brought to public attention, both within the U.S. and on the international stage, prompting other nations to examine the scourge of racism that exists in their own societies. Systemic inequalities, injustices, and shameless racism have become more apparent day by day. Statistics of those contracting and dying from the coronavirus blatantly demonstrate that the virus has been affecting people of color at much higher rates than white people. Because of structural discrimination including lack of access to healthcare resources, fit housing, and cycles of poverty, people of color often have underlying conditions such as diabetes or heart and lung disease and live in dense multigenerational housing, putting them at much higher risk of contracting and dying from the virus. People working on the frontlines of the pandemic—in jobs ranging from "essential work," such as transportation, janitorial and delivery services, and warehouse jobs, to healthcare work and ambulance services—have been disproportionately people of color and immigrants. Mass incarceration, prison overcrowding, and the complete lack of resources provided for prison populations is leading to horrific coronavirus outbreaks within prisons and their surrounding communities, which, again, are disproportionately people of color. According to the NAACP, Black Americans are incarcerated at over five times the rate of white Americans, and although the U.S. represents five percent of the world's population, it has 21 percent of the world's prisoners.[4]

The overwhelming burden of the coronavirus on Black Americans, and people of color more broadly, has been a rude awakening for many Americans who have either turned a blind eye to the country's deep-rooted injustices, or who have been privileged enough to not experience them firsthand—not to mention the absolutely devastating toll it has taken on a large segment of the country's already oppressed population.[5]

Other social conditions have been similarly exacerbated. While domestic and child abuse have always existed, the pandemic created conditions for these social ills to grow. People who were victims of domestic abuse have been trapped at home with their abusers, and because many support systems and resources for survivors of abuse have closed due to the pandemic, people suffering from abuse have nowhere to turn for protection. Isolation and escalating stress also contribute to circumstances that lead to new patterns of domestic violence. Preliminary research has shown that reported cases of domestic abuse have increased by at least 20 percent since the start of the pandemic.[6]

While the coronavirus threatens the physical, social, and economic safety of much of humanity, it is not the only immediate and existential threat. Another massive danger looming over us is climate change. Unlike the pandemic, which is a swiftly moving disaster, climate change is a slow-moving threat wreaking havoc in our world. It is destroying our environment; decimating our way of life; driving uncontrollable migration; and triggering conflict over dwindling land, clean water, food, and energy resources. The members of the United Nations Intergovernmental Panel on Climate Change have been warning us for years that climate change is real, that it is caused by human activity, and that it will result in catastrophic consequences if we do not take immediate and effective action to stop spewing carbon dioxide into the environment. However, we have wasted too much precious time arguing over the reality and causes of climate change.

Meanwhile, the problem has continued growing and we have begun experiencing the harsh results. Some of these consequences were reported in the Global Assessment Report on Biodiversity and Ecosystem Services produced by the Intergovernmental Science-Policy Platform on Biodiversity and Ecosystem Services (IPBES) in the spring of 2019. IPBES chair Sir Robert Watson warned that the report "presents an ominous picture." He went on to say that the "health of ecosystems on which we and all other species depend is deteriorating more rapidly than ever," and that "We are eroding the very foundations of our economies, livelihoods, food security, health and quality of life worldwide." Among other things, the report found that as many as one million plant and animal species are now at risk of extinction.[7]

We only have to look at our increasingly direct experience to know that the report reflects a dismal reality. Consider, for example, the fires that have been ravaging land on different continents. These fires are destroying precious forests including those in the Amazon rainforest and the Congo Basin forest that act as primary and secondary lungs to our world, in that they absorb large quantities of carbon dioxide while producing vast amounts of oxygen, thereby mitigating climate change. Indeed, it is estimated that the Amazon rainforest is one of our most powerful defenses in the fight against climate change as it, alone, pulls billions of tons of carbon dioxide from the air each year.[8] The fires are also destroying large swathes of forests in Siberia, which release far more carbon dioxide into the air than normal forests because they contain peat rich in carbon dioxide that is released into the atmosphere when it burns.[9]

Fires have also raged in California and in Australia, killing wildlife, decimating more forests, destroying homes, threatening human life, and spewing vast quantities of pollution in the air that threaten human health. In Australia alone, the wildfires raging from the end of 2019 to early 2020 burned over 25.5 million acres of land, an area the size of South Korea. The fires are estimated to have killed more than one billion birds, reptiles, and mammals, endangering many unique ecosystems. The air quality index in Australia's capital, Sydney, was reported to be 23 times higher than what is considered hazardous. Increasing levels of dangerous pollution are plaguing cities in many countries including India, France, the United Kingdom, China, and Australia. The levels of pollution are so high that they are seriously affecting the health of the population and interfering with normal human activity such as attending school or walking outside. Moreover, climate change is causing more extreme conditions, less precipitation is leading to longer periods of drought, and drier land and hotter temperatures are turning the land into tinder and making it more susceptible to devastating fires. The dry season is starting earlier, which means that the period of susceptibility to fires is longer.[10]

As though the threat of a global pandemic and the destabilization of the world's economy compounding the havoc wrought by climate change were not enough, the threat of nuclear holocaust still hangs over our heads. Thanks to the vast amount of nuclear weapons the global community has allowed individual countries to amass, the risk of a nuclear holocaust is significant. This kind of existential disaster could easily happen accidentally due to miscalculations caused by escalation and brinkmanship—even if not deliberately. The Doomsday Clock created by the Bulletin of the Atomic Scientists serves as a warning to humanity that it faces impending catastrophe from nuclear war, climate change, and other threats. As of January 2020 it was moved considerably closer to midnight—a mere 100 seconds before global catastrophe.[11]

There are a number of areas in the world that have been prone to escalating tensions that could easily result in a nuclear war—even a limited one. Such escalations include tensions between America and Iran, America and North Korea, and India and Pakistan. Considering the latter, experts have concluded that even if India and Pakistan were to engage in a nuclear war limited in duration and geography it would still have catastrophic consequences. Such a war would result in massive crop failures over a number of years, which, in turn, would subject two billion people to the risk of starvation.[12]

As we observe these various forces at work it is evident that they are increasing in number, frequency, and ferocity, conjuring up the vision of a world that is in the throes of contractions characteristic of arduous and prolonged labor. It is only natural we should ask: What will it give birth to; when will this happen; and do we have a choice in shaping this new creation? These are some of the questions I will explore in this work.

Humanity stands at a critical crossroads. We are faced with a world whose economic, political, social, and religious systems are rapidly unraveling, and that appears to be hurtling toward a dangerous unknown. However, viewing these same circumstances from a different vantage point provides us with an opportunity to change course and choose a more constructive future—a future we truly want and deserve. Indeed, the choices before us are becoming increasingly stark. One of our options is to stick our heads in the sand and stubbornly cling to outworn lenses through which we perceive and interpret our social reality—lenses that not only fail to serve us but that result in increasing self-destruction and unnecessary suffering for a growing mass of humanity.

Alternatively, we can opt to recognize and embrace the fact that we all share a single identity as human beings whose reality encompasses something much greater than our material aspect and our five senses. We can also choose to accept that life on this planet is not accidental but laden with meaning; that we are on a collective journey with a common purpose,[13] which is to create an environment of peace and security in which we can individually and collectively actualize our potential; and that we can choose to exercise our free will choice to adjust our mindsets, and consequently our habits in order to achieve our goals.

While the challenges we face are indeed grave and have the power to destroy us, the greatest danger before us is an utter loss of hope, feelings of deep anxiety, and an increasingly pervasive feeling of helplessness. This hopelessness is born of unbounded fear. This fear is deadly. It is making us lethargic; preventing us from seeing the options before us and from taking vital, sustained, and effective action on all fronts at a time when we most need it; and it is creating in us debilitating anger. In short, it is causing a paralysis of will at a time when we can least afford it. I firmly believe that we can and will overcome these challenges.

However, nothing short of a clear vision of who we want to be, a belief that we can overcome our seemingly intractable challenges, and ceaseless efforts to do so will lead us to the kind of world we all long for and deserve. In this world, peace and security will reign, creating the conditions in which we can fulfill our potential as individuals and as a collective global family. For this to happen, we need to have a collective vision of this new reality and to believe that it is possible. In short, we need to rekindle the dying embers of hope and energize ourselves to take action. Taking that first step of creating unity of thought is essential and is my primary purpose in writing this book.

My second purpose is to demonstrate the necessity of harnessing the greatest human gift, the gift of free will, to achieve our vision of a lasting peace, thereby achieving unity of action. We are in the driver's seat when it comes to determining how quickly it will occur. The sooner we accept that our current systemic, institutional, and individual treatment of human beings and our environment lacks underlying principles such as justice, equity, and oneness, the sooner we can generate meaningful change. Our present patterns and institutions are defunct and no longer serve our wellbeing—it is time for us to alter course. As we do so, we will eventually reduce the scope of our suffering and mitigate its severity.

My third purpose is to propose a roadmap that will get us to peace sooner rather than later. In short, there are two obstacles keeping us from attaining our goal. The first is a set of mindsets encumbered by unexamined limiting beliefs and false assumptions that cause us to interpret events and circumstances of our lives a certain way. These mindsets constitute what I call "inner blocks" because they are generated by our internal perceptions of reality. The second is a set of behaviors that we engage in. Many of these behaviors have ossified into externalized habits that I call "outer blocks." We need to identify our destructive mindsets and habits—our inner and outer blocks—and replace them with new ones that are more constructive. The first step in this map is to identify some key mindsets that keep us from achieving peace and replace them. The second step is to identify some key habits that similarly hinder us from achieving peace and replace them.

By adopting more empowering mindsets and habits we will shift our collective energy from negative to positive, motivating us to act and create the world we want and deserve.

The ideas I propose are the fruits of my reflections on concepts and thoughts I have encountered over a long period, and from a variety of sources and personal inspiration. They include ideas from the field of psychology, political science, core energy coaching, and the writings of the Baha'i Faith. A list of some of these sources can be found in the bibliography at the end of this book. I believe we, as seekers of truth, should seek wisdom wherever we can find it. We should not shy away from seeking it in different sources and trusting in the ability of our inner wisdom to recognize truth when we encounter it, regardless of its source.

Chapter 1

Where We Are Now

TYPICAL REACTION TO CRISES

*O*ur typical reactions to adversities and crises—particularly global ones like the COVID-19 pandemic, the consequent global recession, and climate change—have predominantly fallen into two categories. The first is a sense that we are at the mercy of events beyond our control and that we are victims of our circumstances. We tell ourselves that we are helpless in the face of these realities, and that any action we take, either individually or collectively is futile. These thoughts make us feel hopeless, and consequently apathetic. They also trigger profound fear, anxiety, and depression. The result is that we engage in denial, avoid making decisions, and procrastinate constructive action when we should be applying ourselves energetically to addressing our challenges. In short, we experience a complete paralysis of will. If we do act, we tend to do so too late—and even then only half-heartedly, exacerbating the crisis.

Our current global experience with COVID-19 is a perfect illustration of this mode of reaction. Despite repeated warnings, many international leaders and citizens refused to believe that this was a global emergency that should be met with proactive and timely interventions to reduce the spread of the disease and minimize its casualties. Leaders dithered and procrastinated until the direness of the situation was too painful to ignore. Even once they were forced to act, the measures they took were half-hearted and, essentially, too little, too late. Consequently, when the pandemic hit us with full force, we were woefully unprepared. Inordinate delays in streamlining resources into emergency response action resulted in shortages of masks, ventilators, gloves, and protective equipment for health-care workers, as well as a failure to implement the strict social distancing measures required to avoid community spread of the virus. Meanwhile, the levels of fear and anxiety around the pandemic escalated, resulting in paralysis of action as individuals wondered whether anything they did is of any use.

The second dominant reaction is one of conflict, anger, and frustration. It stems from a mentality that seeks someone else to blame for our misfortune, and it is often accompanied by suspicion, self-righteousness, entitlement, and believing that we are right. The feelings these thoughts engender are ones of anger and defiance, and they often result in conflict and confrontation—all of which lead to disorder and confusion, with potentially catastrophic consequences.

Our experience with the COVID-19 pandemic also illustrates how our habitual reactions based on old, damaging thought patterns play out. We have been quick to label people from other countries such as China, Iran, or Italy as villains in the spread of the virus and to pin blame on the "other." We have shut our borders to other countries out of suspicion. Our fear that resources are scarce have led us to hoard critical supplies and attempt to lock up supplies of potential vaccines. Instead of working collaboratively to ensure the well-being of all, we have been focusing on our own well-being as individuals, states, and nations.

Unfortunately both of these habitual responses of help-lessness and anger are self-destructive. Neither serves us. Not only do they fail to solve the critical challenges we face, but they also exacerbate those problems by paralyzing us at a time when we need to muster all our energies and act urgently as we never have before. According to information collected by the Census Bureau,[14] in the United States alone, a third of the population has been exhibiting signs of clinical anxiety disorder or depressive disorder during the pandemic. In additional research released by the Pew Research Center,[15] 71 percent of the U.S. population is angry about the state of the nation, and 66 percent is fearful. Moreover, these two habitual responses draw us into futile and destructive rounds of blame and confrontation precisely when we need to take responsibility and work collaboratively to find solutions to our common crises. In short, they act as stumbling-blocks on the path toward collective progress and growth.

OLD MINDSET 1: HUMANS ARE EVIL BY NATURE

One of the most self-destructive mindsets that we have nurtured over centuries is that human beings are sinful by nature. Human beings have a strange tendency to look at our past actions, identify behavioral patterns, and succumb to the view that we are doomed to repeat them. Our history is rife with war, territorial aggression, exploitation, and cruelty. Whether on the national or global scale, or in individual interactions, human sin seems to be a common thread. On the individual level, we exploit people's addictions, commit acts of domestic and child abuse, carry out hate crimes, and traffic human beings for material gain. At the national and global level, we create power structures to ensure segments of our populations are disempowered and lack access to necessary resources, commit mass genocides, and use horrific weapons against one another. We look at this seemingly overwhelming evidence and conclude that we are inherently and irredeemably aggressive and cruel. This is the story we have told ourselves about who we are and we have tenaciously clung to it.

We are predisposed to accept this story because of the consistent cross-religious messaging we have received over millennia. The pervasive idea that human beings are naturally inclined to sin—not to mention the concept that we are born carrying the weight of Adam's original sin—have played a significant role in shaping the way we view our nature and instincts. Often, these ideas are inculcated in us from a very young age, and they become fundamental to our understanding of our choices. These ideas are so ingrained in our culture that we are influenced by them whether or not we consciously buy into their religious foundations. Consequently, believing that we are naturally inclined toward sin robs us of a sense of agency in the decisions we make, and we are more likely to make corrupt choices.

When we combine the story we have told ourselves about our propensity to sin with the negative programming prevalent in our culture, it is no surprise that we have concluded that we are incorrigibly aggressive and selfish—it is a permanent feature of who we are and it will not change going forward. Worst of all, we convince ourselves that we cannot change this essential aspect of who we are, and that any attempt to do so is a futile exercise. Instead, we resign ourselves to believing that our future will be a repeat of our past, and that we can neither expect nor hope for anything better.

Such negative self-talk is extremely destructive, and over time it becomes the dominant voice that convinces us that we have always been aggressive, selfish, and prone to violence, that nothing is going to change, and that we are doomed to endlessly repeat our past. Most dangerously, we have come to believe that we do not deserve anything better. Such thoughts result in low self-esteem in individuals, so it is no surprise that internalizing these beliefs about ourselves as a global community has resulted in a gross lack of collective self-esteem that explains a good deal of the destructive behavior we have exhibited over the course of humanity's evolution to date.

OLD MINDSET 2: WE ARE VICTIMS OF UNCONTROLLABLE EVENTS AND PURPOSELESS SUFFERING

Another self-destructive thought pattern we have adopted is the perspective that we are being whiplashed by global crises that are causing deep and meaningless suffering. One of the hallmarks of the time we live in is the pervasive and discomforting feeling that, as individuals, we are at the mercy of uncontrollable and seemingly random events. The unexpectedness and severity of the coronavirus pandemic and the rapidly accelerating evidences of climate change are two current crises that we consider to be happening randomly to us, with effects beyond our control. We feel powerless and bewildered in the face of these crises because they do not fit with our conceptualization of how reality should unfold. Our powerlessness heightens our feelings that our suffering is purposeless.

A fundamental operating concept that exists both on the individual and societal level, and that we cling to as if it represents an objective truth about our lives, is the belief that human beings are guaranteed a degree of certainty and stability in life. As a result, we come to expect the flow of stability and refuse to accept the possibility of any interruption in it. We believe that if we follow a particular path, then we are entitled to certain outcomes. We have become inordinately attached to those outcomes and the process by which we expect to receive them. One particularly detrimental manifestation of this pattern is in habits of materialism, for example, the natural progression of education to the entitlement of economic benefit. Supposedly, if you apply yourself and study hard in school, then you should get good grades that will allow you to find a stable job and achieve a certain lifestyle of comfort. This philosophy similarly promises that if you save money, you will be protected against any challenge in keeping a roof over your head and food on the table. Yet, during a pandemic that has triggered a global economic recession, all of these assumptions and entitlements have gone up in smoke. Naturally, when crises like the pandemic snatch away the outcomes we have worked so hard to guarantee for ourselves and that we feel entitled to receiving, we feel defeated and hopeless.

Another fallout from this entitled mode of thinking is the complete abdication of responsibility for any negative eventualities that arise. We assume that, since we followed the set path supposedly leading to stability, we cannot be at fault for any negative consequences—regardless of whether these consequences directly stem from our own previous mistakes or bad decisions. Denial sets in as we distance our-selves from these repercussions and refuse to take responsi-bility for them. Seeing these negative events as distinct from our own choices, we interpret them as uncontrollable and beyond our reach. Having convinced ourselves of our utter lack of agency, we passively resign ourselves to the detrimen-tal effects of the situation and wallow in our hopelessness.

We have followed this exact thought process in response to both the coronavirus pandemic and climate change. In pursuing our materialist ambitions—the path that was sup-posed to lead to comfort and satisfy material greed—we have generated severe and harmful effects on our environ-ment that have led to both crises. However, we refuse to see the negative impacts our actions have caused, and we there-fore feel that they are occurring arbitrarily and that we have no control over them.

OLD MINDSET 3: HUMANITY HAS IRREVOCABLY FAILED

Another pattern we have that does not serve us well is wilting in the face of perceived failure. Our tendency to think in terms of mistakes we have made and to beat our-selves up over them is another reason we become hopeless rather than looking for the lessons we can learn and opting to try different approaches. As we confront the twin global challenges of coronavirus and climate change, we find that our leaders and societies are spectacularly failing to address them. This incapacity is certainly not what we expected of ourselves as a modern, sophisticated society. Our perceived failure has caused us to become disillusioned, which has compounded our paralysis. The reason we feel this way is because we define success as the realization of a particular goal or outcome—for example, finding a speedy and effective solution to the pandemic and climate change.

Moreover, we have the habit of linking our self-worth to outcomes we expect to achieve. Failure to achieve those outcomes induces feelings of low self-worth and depression. The mental process we engage in is akin to that of an individual who applies for a job and sets their heart on being hired, planning out a whole life based on their acceptance. When they find out they were not hired, not only is their plan thrown of course, but their dreams are shattered. The self worth they had tied to getting the job disintegrates, and they are left hopeless, helpless, and unconfident.

Similarly, we tell ourselves that we are on a downward slide from which we can never recover; there is no hope for the world going forward. Our future is dark. The best we can hope to do is to mitigate the disasters we have unleashed, tolerate them, and adapt to them as best we can, recognizing that we must settle for what little is possible given that we will never have the kind of world we want and deserve.

OUR CURRENT STATE:
HOPELESSNESS AND INACTION

Believing that human beings are intrinsically evil, that we are victims of incessant and meaningless suffering, or that we have massively failed to protect ourselves from existential crises, leads to feeling despondent, and futile. These feelings in turn rob us of our energy and naturally incline us toward apathy and lethargy. Consequently, when we most urgently need to act we dither and vacillate between paths of action. When we finally act, our endeavor is not only late but also insufficient, further compounding our difficulties.

Eventually, we simply give up and sink into complete inaction, having lost all sense of agency in our lives.

These mindsets are currently affecting every facet of human existence. We observe them playing out in our physical lives in our response to the coronavirus pandemic. Despite the warnings issued by scientists starting in 2007, ending with the warning issued by the World Health Organization in 2018 that a global pandemic was inevitable and could occur at any time,[16] world leaders largely failed to prepare and act.[17]

Consequently, we were caught flat-footed. Even once it became apparent that the coronavirus was likely to become a pandemic, governments dragged their heels. They failed to provide their citizens and health care workers with adequate masks, personal protective equipment, and ventilators. They largely failed to impose measures such as social distancing, lock-downs, and mask-wearing early enough. In the handful of countries where early action was taken, the effects of the pandemic were milder. In many places, measures that were imposed too late were lifted too early, demonstrating a lack of decisiveness and commitment to a plan.

We also see the effect of these mindsets on the environment in our response to climate change. As with the pandemic, scientists have been warning us for years that we need to take action early to forestall catastrophic consequences to our environment. After much deliberation and wringing of hands we finally came up with a system of pledges under the Paris Agreement, aiming to mitigate greenhouse gas emissions and limit global temperature increases. Yet even as we finally took action, we resorted to half-measures. The pledges are voluntary with no system of enforcement to back them up. Worst yet, even if they are fulfilled to the letter, they do not go far enough in fore-stalling the worst consequences of climate change. Instead of accepting the truth that ignoring a problem will not make it go away and taking the opportunity to be decisive and avoid such consequences, we have put off taking action as long as possible until the pain induced by our circumstances becomes so bad that we must act.

Our mindsets also affect our economy as we struggle to address the global economic recession. Although we know from the global economic crisis of 2008 that the only way to resolve such a crisis is for governments to come together and work collaboratively to solve it, we have become com-placent and have not begun to work cooperatively toward finding a solution before we have endured deep suffering.

Lastly, our mindsets play out in our reactions to the social injustices we have created. We have known for decades that systemic injustices like racism, sexism, and queer-phobia are entrenched features of our societal struc-tures around the world. Despite repeated cries for change in order to alleviate the suffering of those negatively impacted, we have failed to make the radical changes necessary. People are losing patience. They are reaching their limit and are now in the streets protesting structural racism in the United States and around the world. How much turmoil ensues will depend on how quickly governments choose to respond to these pleas for justice.

In each instance, whether physical, environmental, eco-nomic, or social, the ultimate result of these mindsets has been paralysis of will and lack of effective and timely action.

Chapter 2

Reframing Our Mindset: The Peace Alchemy Method

THE MATURATION ANALYSIS: HUMANITY'S TRANSITION FROM ADOLESCENCE TO MATURITY

*R*ather than allowing these mindsets to paralyze us into inaction and blind us to the choices we can make to tackle our challenges, we can reframe the way we perceive our current realities to infuse us with the energy and hope we need to create a better world. Instead of lamenting our victimhood, inherent evil, or perceived failure, we can choose to understand our current social reality as a collective humanity against the backdrop of the history of our collective evolution. From its inception, humanity as a whole has gone through stages of growth akin to the developmental stages experienced by an individual. Just as an individual passes through stages of infancy, childhood, and adolescence before attaining the age of maturity, so too, have we successfully passed through the early stages of development, and we now stand at the threshold of maturity. These stages were characterized by the expanding circles of societal unity and integration starting with the family unit, advancing to the tribe, and later progressing to the city-state and the nation.

Currently, we are in the throes of a turbulent, pre-maturity adolescence in which we are acting out and exhibiting some atrocious behavior. Just as a loving parent who has perspective on their child's growth understands that their teenager's rebellion is a phase that will pass, so, too, must we have the wisdom and patience to know that our current phase of rebellion will pass. The loving parent does not give up on their teenager and throw them out of the house. Rather, they provide persistent guidance and point out better choices that the teenager can make. Even though humanity seems to be very attached to nationalism, xenophobia, and unilateralism, these behaviors are signs of our current immaturity, and they will eventually pass. They do not describe who we are in our essence and we should not view them as indictments of us as human beings. We can trust that with time, patience, and consistent effort to make better choices, we will break out of these cycles of selfishness and choose to widen our circle of integration to encompass the whole human race.

At this stage we will recognize that our primary loyalty is to humanity as a whole and that other loyalties, including national loyalties, are secondary. In this context our current stage can be seen as presaging our collective coming-of-age. We are ready to develop new capacities, moral standards, and institutions that we will need as we take the next inevitable step toward maturity. This maturity will be marked by the unification of the planet into one organic, global community of nations, served by global institutions fit to meet our needs and resolve our challenges for the 21st century and beyond. This step represents the consummation of our collective social evolution. As U.N. Secretary-General António Guterres has reminded us, we could view our history since the birth of the United Nations as one that is divided into several parts. For a time we lived in a bipolar world marked by cold-war rivalry between the Soviet Union and America. This period was followed by a unipolar one in which the United States was the unchallenged world power. We are now in a period of chaos which he believes will lead us eventually to a multipolar world.[18] Another way to interpret this history is that we have been going through a process of collective growth and experimentation that will eventually lead us to a multipolar world in which the oneness of nations is recognized. How quickly we arrive there is a matter of how intelligently and wisely we exercise our power to choose our future.

Viewed through this lens, it is no wonder that we are acting out and flirting with dangerous and extreme behaviors. We are not incorrigibly evil, selfish and aggressive, nor are we doomed to repeat our immature mistakes of the past, we are simply figuring out what it takes to get from this present tumultuous stage to the stage of collective maturity, and in the process, we are discovering latent capacities and powers. In fact, what we are experiencing and witnessing should be viewed as a distortion of the human spirit rather than a reflection of its reality. We can be optimistic knowing that this phase will pass and we will find that we are capable of creating a peaceful and dynamic social system that affords us the environment in which we can fulfill our individual and collective potential.

One of the key challenges before us is to ensure that we do not linger in this collective developmental phase of adolescence for an inordinately long period of time. Doing so will only cause us to retard our growth, which essentially translates into prolonged and unnecessary suffering. We have already begun to see evidences of such suffering in the growing multiplicity, intensity, and complexity of the global challenges that we are confronting—challenges such as climate change, the COVID-19 pandemic, global economic crises, nuclear proliferation and the resurgent threat of nuclear war, unprecedented migration, terrorism, genocide, and other gross human rights abuses. As we will see later, it is within our capacity to actively engage our power of choice and consult, collaborate, and cooperate together to find new and more constructive ways of building the world we want and deserve.

THE PHOENIX EFFECT: PARALLEL PROCESSES OF DISINTEGRATION AND INTEGRATION

This period leading to the advent of humanity's maturity is characterized by two parallel processes of disintegration and integration. As our immature, selfish past reaches its peak and begins to fade away, our cohesive, mature nature starts to emerge. This simultaneous process of death and rebirth is occurring like a caterpillar undergoes metamorphosis to transform into a butterfly.[19]

The caterpillar starts by consuming large volumes of food. As it does so, it grows so much that it has to shed its skin, a process known as "molting." It then proceeds to consume ever-larger quantities of food and repeats this sequence of molting and eating several times over. This process is reminiscent of humanity's rapid development, coupled with a rapid consumption of resources including food, water, and energy. As we hit the ceiling of our growth, we shed our old ways and find new ways of being that allow us to consume even more. If we find that our water wells are running dry at ten feet, we bore deeper ones reaching down fifty feet or a hundred feet.

Eventually, the caterpillar reaches the limit of what it can achieve as an earth-bound caterpillar. At this point it forms a cocoon around itself and begins to excrete enzymes that literally start to dissolve and consume its body. This process of the caterpillar's disintegration is akin to the process we have been witnessing in human society for a while now. Like the caterpillar, we have voraciously consumed finite resources in our quest to acquire greater material comforts. In the process of feeding our insatiable appetite we have polluted our environment to such a degree that it has set off a chain of disastrous consequences as reflected in extreme droughts, fires, floods, and other environmental manifestations of climate change. Our insatiable appetite has triggered a process of disintegration that has gained particular momentum with the advent of the coronavirus pandemic. Having hit the limits of what we can achieve with our outmoded systems, institutions, and laws in all spheres—political, economic, health, environmental, and religious—we are now watching all of these systems collapse as they prove unequal to the task of serving the needs of humanity at this stage of our collective growth in the 21st century and beyond.

However, hidden from sight within the cocoon, there is another process taking place. This essential process is performed by small clusters of cells called imaginal discs that are latent within the caterpillar from the beginning of its existence. During the cocooning stage, each cluster begins to grow a particular part of what will eventually become the emerging butterfly. While the number of cells in each of these clusters is initially small, the cells begin to multiply rapidly. This process occurs at the same time as the enzymes are consuming the remaining portions of the caterpillar. Similarly, in our world there are clusters of human beings that have been tirelessly working toward the creation of a unified world in which the principle of the oneness of humanity is recognized as one of the laws governing social reality. These clusters serve the interests of all of humanity regardless of national, ethnic, racial, gender, economic, or class difference, and they are driven by a desire to love and serve all human beings. An example of such a cluster is the growing number of global civil society organizations that are actively collaborating together in a quest to achieve world peace. Another is the global movement toward reforming the United Nations to make it more democratic and fit to respond to the challenges of this century. Yet another is the growing worldwide movement to protest for the elimination of racism.

Finally, when the time is right and the butterfly is fully formed, it slowly breaks out of its cocoon and emerges as a magnificent new creation of a higher order; whereas the caterpillar was earth-bound and therefore limited in both its vision and capacities, the butterfly can fly, and consequently, its capacity surpasses that of the caterpillar. Moreover, its horizons are broader and its perspectives greater. So, too, the time will come when the process of the disintegration of our current systems will come to an end, along with all the attendant mess it produces. Meanwhile, we will have simultaneously developed new capacities, tools, and moral standards that we need to serve us in this stage of our emerging maturity.

We have already begun to witness early glimmerings of such capacities and powers in the growing calls for global consultation, cooperation, solidarity, and collaboration. Scientists took the lead in role modeling how this could be done as they collaborated tirelessly to find a vaccine to protect us from the disease caused by COVID-19. In doing so, they demonstrated the enormous benefits to humanity of setting aside the artificial barriers based on ego and antiquated ideas of nationalism.

Leaders in the sphere of governance have also begun to call for multilateralism and solidarity on a scale hitherto unmatched. Dr. Henry Kissinger has noted that no one country can single-handedly overcome the virus. He has asserted that "addressing the necessities of the moment must ultimately be coupled with a global collaborative vision and program," emphasizing the need for a unified approach in tackling the pandemic.[20] Meanwhile the Secretary-General of the United Nations, António Guterres, has raised the clarion call for a massive, multilateral response based on "shared responsibility and global solidarity" to build a better world.[21] He urges us to remember that "we are only as strong as the weakest health system in our interconnected world," and he asserts his belief that our world has irrevocably changed, saying,"We can go back to the world as it was before or deal decisively with those issues that make us all unnecessarily vulnerable to crises."

By choosing to view our current experience through this lens we can make the most of our current tests and meet them with greater hope, confidence, and positive energy. The process is very messy but the outcome is glorious. Indeed, like the butterfly coming out of its cocoon, it leads to new creation of a higher level.

The first part of this process involves the disintegration of outworn institutions, policies, and habits that no longer serve the well-being of humanity. This disintegration has become increasingly evident in the collapse of social, political, religious, and economic systems—the signs have been all around us. The recurring instances of genocide worldwide we, as a global community have been unable to stop; the continuing proliferation of nuclear arms that we have also been powerless to arrest; the seemingly intractable challenge of climate change that we have been unwilling to properly tackle; the spread of lawlessness and terrorism leading to the collapse of law and order and the phenomenon of failed states; the resulting waves of migration caused by people fleeing their homelands in quest of safety and repose; repeated financial crises culminating in the global economic crisis of 2008; and the recurring threats of a pandemic are some of the most salient of these signs. As the process of collapse accelerates, so our trust in our failing systems and institutions plummets. Despite the plethora of signs, we have not truly been paying attention, preferring to stick our heads in the sand and hold on to our outworn yet comfortable mindsets and habits. However, the disintegrative process is relentless; it is rapidly gaining momentum and will not be ignored. It is steadily sweeping away the barriers and blocks to our growth and making way for new processes of collaboration and cooperation. To ignore it and fail to adjust ourselves to the reality that our systems are bankrupt is to invite increasing mental and physical suffering. The COVID-19 pandemic and its twin calamity, the damage it is wreaking on our global economic system, have further accelerated the decline. In the process of doing so, they are rudely yet effectively removing the scales from our eyes and stirring our conscience. We are beginning to become aware of the serious defects of our societal infrastructure and the need to completely reconceptualize and reorganize our social affairs.

The second part of the twin processes that we are experiencing is the process of integration. It is particularly evident in all the marvelous movements we are currently witnessing that call for constructing a happier, more peaceful and secure society, in which the nobility of every human being is acknowledged regardless of race, gender, faith, education, means, or class. A hallmark of this integrative process is the willingness—and beyond that, the desire—to consult and collaborate to bring into being new and viable social structures that serve the well-being of human beings everywhere and allow us all to fulfill our individual and collective potential. Examples of these constructive movements are the collaborative and vigorous efforts poured into finding ways to arrest global warming, mitigate it damages, and adapt to changes that are irreversible; the outpourings of solidarity expressed in the Me Too movement, designed to raise consciousness about and create solidarity against the sexual harassment and abuse of women worldwide; similar expressions of solidarity to protect and uphold the dignity of Black lives in the Black Lives Matter movement; and the strong impetus from civil society to propose changes to the United Nations system to make it fit to address the global challenges and needs of the 21st century and beyond.

THE ROLE OF SUFFERING

When we take a step back and look at the global crises the world has been experiencing for many years now, we notice a distinctive pattern. The crises are multiplying in number, frequency, and intensity, yielding a similar intensification of suffering. This pattern is reminiscent of contractions during labor, which build and escalate until they bring forth the birth of a wonderful new creation. Through the pain and suffering, life is born. Similarly, the world is currently in labor and is about to give birth to a new way of being, a new global order that will be characterized by an awareness and acceptance of foundational principles and values to govern our international lives. This new order will be governed by a set of global institutions that are built upon and reflect these principles and that are fit to serve our collective interests at this stage of our global maturity. Our collective suffering helps to develop the capacities necessary to attain this next level in our societal evolution.

Testing of Strengths and Weaknesses

One of the purposes of suffering is to serve as a stress test for our social systems—a collective test designed to make us aware of both our strengths and weaknesses. The global pandemic alone is already exposing many weaknesses in our societies and governance systems around the world. The scales have been rudely stripped from our eyes, revealing the deficiency of health care systems; the absence of social safety nets; the inordinate disparity between the rich and the poor; the entrenchment of racism and discrimination in the structures of society; the bankruptcy of leadership; and the absence of vital global systems of cooperation, collaboration, and collective decision-making and enforcement, to name but a few. This test is prompting us to begin taking the steps necessary to achieve a much greater future society than the one we are experiencing, a future in which the oneness of humanity will become the operational principle of international life and will constitute the foundation of, and be reflected in, the institutional, legal, social, and policy infrastructures of our world.

Instilling of Leadership Responsibility

Suffering can also serve the important purpose of instilling within the leaders of a new age the appropriate sense of responsibility they must be willing to take on. In the wake of the COVID-19 pandemic and the worsening global economic crisis, we are already beginning to see the first glimmerings of awareness on the part of people everywhere that we owe it to ourselves to elect leaders that possess certain essential qualities, chief among them honesty, trustworthiness, competence, compassion, and the ability to put aside ego and act tirelessly and selflessly in service to the people of the world.[22] Beyond that, we are also learning the importance of investigating the character and motivations of potential candidates before we cast our ballots. We will return to this topic later in this work when we explore leadership in more detail.

Fusion of a Divided Society

The pain and heat generated by suffering also fuse the disparate segments of our global society into one organically unified, indivisible, global community. A prime example of the salutary effects of suffering is the experience of the United States during the Civil War. While the war was brutal and caused untold suffering and pain, it ultimately welded the disparate and contending American states together and established the unity of this nation.

Radical Reconceptualization of Society

Suffering also disillusions us, stirs our conscience, and ultimately instills in us the resolve to bring about a radical change in our very conception of society, inspiring us to see it as a single, indivisible whole that is organically united. Our experience with the coronavirus pandemic, although brief, is already creating a growing awareness that we are all in this together, that our 193 countries are cabins on a ship navigating the seas of international life, as beautifully described by former president of the U.N. Security Council Kishore Mahbubani. When storms like the pandemic hit, our only chance of survival is to have a competent captain and crew at the helm whose sole purpose is to serve the denizens of all of the cabins. If each cabin creates a contingency plan of its own without working together cooperatively, not only will we not survive, but such actions are likely to sink the ship. We are slowly learning that our only hope of surviving the pandemic and the global economic crisis is to collaborate, consult, and act collectively. We need a universal set of marching orders by which all nations are willing to abide, and that reflect the best practices and scientific knowledge about what to do to avoid the spread of the virus. We need to have a central body responsible for assessing each nation's needs for personal protective equipment, ventilators, disinfectant, antidotes and vaccines to treat a pandemic, and that is authorized to require production and equitable distribution of these vital resources. We need international consultation and coordination of steps to protect vulnerable people from inordinate economic hardship and ensure that everyone has access to basic necessities like food and water. These are all lessons that we are being forced to learn, thanks to the pandemic. In this sense the pandemic can be viewed as a blessing in disguise, exposing the many ways in which our local, national, and international systems have been sorely wanting and giving us the opportunity of making the shifts necessary for our well-being.

Infusion of New Capacities and Powers

The suffering we are experiencing is also infusing in us the capacity, virtues, principles, and tools we need to take the next step in our collective evolution toward a global system of governance strongly founded on a set of shared global ethics. Another way to think of it is by considering what happens to a piece of iron when it is subjected to the intense heat of the forge. The iron starts off being hard and cold. The heat of the fire eventually causes it to become red-hot and malleable, capable of being cast in new shapes. So, too, do the fires of adversity, ordeals, and intense suffering cause us to give up lower qualities like selfishness, prejudice, nationalism, and isolationism that no longer serve us for more ennobling qualities of oneness and unity. More will be said about this system and the principles underlying it in the section of this work that discusses a new system of global governance.

Creation of Spiritual Awareness

Finally, suffering can serve as a catalyst inviting us to a deeper understanding of who we really are as human beings, what our purpose is, the social laws and principles that govern our existence, and ways we can craft social, political, economic, and religious institutions that honor and reflect that reality. Indeed, what if this suffering is merely a portal beckoning and inviting us to go deeper and discover that we are fundamentally and primarily spiritual beings experiencing a physical reality rather than the opposite? It can be a motivating force helping us to understand that the way we have come to perceive ourselves and others represents only the tip of the iceberg of who we truly are. Similar to the tip of the iceberg, the material aspects of our lives represent at best a small fraction of our reality as human beings. The bulk of who we are is not as obvious and it requires exploration. Human beings often come to an understanding of what we want and need by being deprived of it. It is only after we experience the absence of something that we appreciate that thing when we attain it.[23]

This is true of darkness and light, hunger and nourishment, poverty and wealth; light can only be appreciated as a counterpart and relief from darkness, and so on. It is just as true with respect to spiritual deprivation and the recognition and development of our spiritual capacities. What if our current suffering is the necessary material darkness demonstrating the need for the light of our true spirituality? Albert Camus illustrates the arrival at this deep understanding in these lines, "In the depth of winter, I finally learned that within me, there lay, an invincible summer."[24]

Consciousness of Our Oneness

Far from marking the end of human civilization as we know it, our current global experiences are preparing humanity for a new stage in its growth by virtue of their equalizing effect that awakens within us the awareness of our oneness and equality, thus providing us with a valuable launching-pad for a leap in collective growth. These crises act as a catalyst to release the potential inherent in human beings, the inherent nobility and excellence of our reality, and the full measure of our collective destiny on earth.

We are already beginning to see the first signs of this reality. The virus is teaching us that we are all one, regardless of race, gender, creed, education, or wealth. Even though the pandemic is currently impacting oppressed communities at a disproportionate rate, over the longer term we will find that we are all impacted by it in serious ways given the level of our interconnectedness. As lockdowns continue causing an increasing number of businesses to fail and farms to lose crops because of the shortage of farmworkers; as our supply chains continue to be interrupted; as our schools remain closed, depriving young folks of a crucial education and causing a sizeable fraction of the work-force, disproportionately women, to stay home; as the value of stocks and wealth continues to plummet, our economic life will be impacted to such a degree that we will all feel the pain. Until we are able to stamp the virus out worldwide none of us will ever be safe as the virus makes its repeated rounds.

We Stand or Fall Together

We are slowly starting to realize that we stand or fall together. Not one of us is safe until we are all safe. Moreover, we all have similar hopes for security and self-fulfillment and we are all plagued by similar human fears and vulnerabilities. The key to thriving as a human race is for us to collaborate and cooperate with good will and in a spirit of harmony to achieve the well-being of all. Our scientists are demonstrating this spirit of collaboration and good will by putting aside their egos and desire for individual recognition, discarding competition, sharing their findings, and collaborating on a vital endeavor to find a vaccine for the COVID-19 virus to save the lives of human beings, no matter who or where they are. In the past, scientific research was marked by intense competition and a culture of secrecy as scientists jealously guarded the results of their research until they could get their work published in reputable journals and garner academic credit. However, there has recently been a seismic shift in research culture. Large amounts of data are now being released daily by preprint servers that did not even exist a decade ago, allowing research to progress at an unprecedented clip as scientists use online platforms such as Slack and Twitter to analyze these materials.[25]

Moreover, due to the speed with which it is spreading, the coronavirus is affording us a much-needed and timely opportunity to rapidly learn how to collaborate on finding solutions as an interconnected world community. We are going to need these skills if we are to address the other looming disaster of climate change in a timely fashion—before it completely destroys us. In some ways, one might view the pandemic and global economic crisis it has provoked as a dress-rehearsal for climate change. While the world has been unwilling to recognize the degree of threat posed by global warming—despite the ever-increasing evidence of the damage it wreaks—and it has been dithering in taking the collective steps necessary to arrest the process, the pandemic and the economic crisis are by their very nature designed to get our immediate attention and to focus our minds and energies toward finding rapid solutions. The lessons we learn here will prove to us that we can work as one to tackle global challenges, and they will consequently stand us in excellent stead in confronting the deeper and more severe problem of climate change.

THE OPPORTUNITY ADVANTAGE: RECOGNIZING THE POSSIBILITIES FOR GROWTH INHERENT IN OUR TEMPORARY FAILURES

The key to harnessing the opportunities in our temporary failure lies in our ability to shift our focus from an outcome orientation to a growth orientation—in other words, looking for the progress and growth we can achieve as a result of the hard lessons we are learning, rather than focusing on short-term outcomes like the apparent health of the stock market on any given day. Shawn Achor, bestselling author of *The Happiness Advantage: How a Positive Brain Fuels Success in Work and Life,* writes, "Study after study shows that if we are able to conceive of a failure as an opportunity for growth, we are all the more likely to experience that growth."[26] He adds that we become short-sighted when we are faced with obstacles, and that we tend to either repeat more of the same behavior that got us into difficulty in the first place, wishfully hoping for a different outcome, or we slide back, giving up on the progress we have made and truly setting ourselves back. Consequently, he says that "when we are stressed or in crisis, many people miss the most important path of all: the path up."[27]

We observe both of these negative tendencies at work in our early attempts to deal with the COVID-19 pandemic—countries have been narrowly focused on their self-interest, putting their own people above the well-being of other nations, and failing to recognize that we all will sink or swim together. Meanwhile, the reality is that the virus knows no borders and we are only as safe as our weakest link. In some countries leaders have taken this opportunity to tighten their grip-like power. In Hungary, for instance, hard-won progress has been rolled back as parliament has been disbanded and President Viktor Orban has been given authority to issue any decree he pleases.

Yet, there is an alternate path that requires that we neither repeat dysfunctional behavior nor regress. Achor suggests that in situations of failure there is always a third way that few opt for, yet that is the only viable way out. He says we should use the downward momentum of failure to catapult ourselves in an entirely new direction. This type of course-altering action calls for a new level of thinking, as illustrated by the famous statement attributed to Albert Einstein, "We cannot solve our problems with the same thinking we used when we created them." It requires believing that each problem we face bears a gift that allows us to grow even more. Our job is to find those opportunities for growth and wholeheartedly seize them.

Chapter 3

Mindsets and Habits

WHAT IS MINDSET AND WHY IT MATTERS

*I*f we were to conceive of our world as a garden, we would notice that the reason why our garden is not flourishing as it should be is because the flowers we plant—our constructive endeavors and attempts at creating a better world—are often strangled by the weeds of our disempowering beliefs, perceptions, and interpretations of reality, before these flowers have a chance to grow. To give the garden a chance to thrive, we must first remove these habitual, destructive mindsets.

Our mindset is caused by repetitive and unconscious thoughts and emotional reactions that drive us and create our reality. These thoughts and emotions, in turn, result from the lens through which we view, understand, and interpret what is happening around us. For the individual, that lens is shaped by our past experiences, beliefs, cultures, and family influences. Similarly, societies—whether local, national, or global—interpret their collective experience through the lens of their past experiences, their dominant beliefs, and their values.

The greatest single factor shaping our individual or collective lenses is the way we choose to interpret our experiences—nothing has meaning until we assign it meaning. These interpretations become our habitual thoughts and beliefs. As more individuals adopt these thoughts and beliefs they start to form the culture of a society, and over time these become ossified and unconscious. Even though we stop being aware that they are there, they continuously run in the background of our minds, influencing every decision or course of action we take. In this sense they are like the operating system of a computer that is always running in the background even though we are not conscious of its influence as we use it for our daily work. As time passes, we begin unwittingly identifying ourselves with our largely unconscious system of beliefs about reality.

Moreover, these habitual thoughts give rise to emotions that subsequently determine our behavior. In turn, our behavior, which is based on the choices we make, determines our reality. To the extent that we are caught in the grip of negative individual and collective mindsets, we will experience negative feelings, resulting in either ineffective or destructive action.

An example of how our thoughts lead to mindsets that cause negative behaviors is the way the global community responded to the COVID-19 pandemic. It quickly became clear that states needed to acquire enough personal protective equipment and ventilators in order to keep their health workers and citizens safe during the pandemic. The dominant thought in response to this crisis was that these resources would be scarce. In turn, this mindset evoked a deep feeling of fear, and even panic. Fear then provoked states to take whatever steps they deemed necessary to lock up these essential resources for their own citizens. On one occasion an airplane that had been filled with face masks requested by the French government was sitting on the tarmac in China waiting to leave for France, when it was suddenly diverted to the United States because the U.S. had offered to pay a higher cash price for the cargo.[28] Moreover, this negative progression of thought, feeling, and action led to an unprecedented situation in which governors of states in the U.S. were bidding against each other in an effort to secure these critical supplies, even though they were parts of a single nation that should have been acting in unison through federal response.[29]

Had nations instead adopted the mindset that they had the power to create an abundance of supplies and that their fortunes were dependent on one another's success because of their inherent oneness, they would have generated the energy and resources necessary. Rather than immediately responding out of fear and competing with each other, they could have collaborated and ramped up global manufacturing of critical supplies and created a system to ensure their equitable distribution worldwide.

It follows that if we do not like the results we are experiencing in our global society, it is crucial that we bring our habitual thoughts to the surface so that we can explore them and decide which of them serve us and which do not. Once we are aware of them we can meaningfully exercise our free will choice to keep them, modify them, or completely dispense with them, perhaps replacing them with a more constructive and empowering set of thoughts and messages. By changing the way we look at reality and interpret it, we can begin the process of changing our experience for the better. As self-help author and motivational speaker Wayne Dyer observed insightfully, "When you change the way you look at things, the things you look at change."[30]

If we do not like a world that is fraught with insecurity and conflict, we can opt for a new way of looking at who we are, what gives our life meaning, and what we want to experience that is more likely to yield a peaceful and secure world.

Now that we have seen the power of shifting our mindset to generate energy and hope, broaden our range of choices and reactions, and ultimately shift our behavior to more positive and constructive actions, we can apply this process to several other dominant mindsets that have held back humanity's progress and collective development.

REPLACING THE HABITS THAT KEEP US FROM PEACE

Once we are clear that we are committed to creating a peaceful and secure world in which we can fulfill our individual and collective potential, and we have removed the inner blocks to creating that world by changing our mindset, the next step is to identify the outworn habits and behaviors we need to change to achieve our goal. If our old mindsets act as inner blocks to creating a peaceful world, then our dysfunctional behaviors and habits can be viewed as the outer blocks that similarly prevent us from achieving our goal.

Before we begin identifying these habits and exploring empowering replacements for each of them, we must first have the courage to own up to the truth that institutions, political and economic theories, social assumptions, laws, and policies are there to serve the welfare of humanity. If they cease doing so, we must have no compunction about abandoning them—regardless of how vaunted or well-crafted they are—in favor of more constructive alternatives, rather than sacrificing ourselves to uphold them.[31]

Having mustered the courage to act, we need to commit ourselves wholeheartedly to the task at hand. Without commitment there will be no follow-through and we will likely give up as soon as we face the first signs of difficulty or resistance. Sustained courage and commitment are essential to creating the capabilities we need to succeed. As we build these capabilities we will develop a collective confidence and we will want to commit to additional behaviors and habits that bring us peace and security. This commitment, coupled with courage, will spawn further capabilities and lead to deeper confidence.

Some among you might be skeptical that such a thing is possible. To you I commend the views of the famous 20th century world historian Arnold Toynbee on the subject of collective habits. He posited that humanity was going to have to choose between "political unity" and complete self-destruction. He observed that there was incredible resistance to the idea of political unity, but he went on to say that such resistance was no more than a social habit. The good news, he added, was that just as habits could be acquired, they could also be modified and relinquished. He was confident that we will eventually abandon the habit of refusing political unity, which he coined the "great refusal," as soon as it becomes clear that clinging to it will pose an existential threat to humanity. Refusing political unity would effectively mean choosing death. Moreover, he predicted that humanity will be able to replace its destructive habit with constructive ones very quickly when faced with the grim reality of an existential crisis.[32]

Our experience with the COVID-19 pandemic is demonstrating how accurate his prediction was. We have had to radically change behaviors—from not engaging in physical closeness with friends and loved ones to cancelled vacations and remote work and school. We have had to quickly train ourselves to wear masks when stepping outside, wash hands frequently, and be vigilant about maintaining a distance of six feet from those who do not live in our household. Beyond these more mundane shifts, we have been forced to consider new ways of conducting political and social life, including holding elections. Some athletes who were unable to engage in their professions thought of ways to use their skills to help others. A striking example of this was a professional boxer who decided to teach boxing to staff at a hospital as a means of helping them destress. Some celebrities similarly turned their attentions toward acts of service, including giving free concerts to keep people's spirits up or reading bedtime stories to children to afford their parents a break from long, gruelling days. If we can adapt to such draconian and invasive changes so quickly, surely we are capable of making more moderate and sustained changes necessary to mitigate and arrest global warming and climate change, to put an end to war and flagrant human rights abuses, to eliminate weapons of mass destruction, and to create a more equitable global economy in which the extremes of wealth and poverty no longer exist.

We have already experienced the tremendous power we derive from shifting our mindset by reframing our interpretation of our nature as human beings and our current global state of affairs using more positive and empowering perspectives. When we view circumstances through the lens of a negative mindset we feel helpless, apathetic, and ultimately paralyzed into inaction. However, once we adopt a new, more positive way of interpreting our reality we are filled with hope. We feel empowered, energized, and motivated to take action, believing that we are captains of our ship and masters of our destiny. We are willing to try different approaches to achieving peace, understanding that we may fail many times before we succeed. Yet, we are not deterred. Our new perspective makes us more courageous and confident. We reclaim the sense of agency we have in our own lives and recognize that our future is dependent upon the choices we make going forward rather than the past choices that brought us to the unhappy and unsatisfactory state where we are now.

Chapter 4

The Power of Choice

here is an art to making constructive choices. It requires us to recognize that at every moment in our collective lives we have the opportunity to assess where we are, envision where we want to be, and then harness the power of free will to take steps in bridging that gap. First we must accept the reality of where we are and how we got there fully and without judgment. We must also be willing to accept responsibility for our part in creating our current situation, acknowledge that our old methods no longer serve us, and recognize that it is time to make radical changes. To quote the famous poet William Ernest Henley, "I am the master of my fate: I am the captain of my soul."[33] It is only once we take these steps that we become creative and we begin to see a broader array of choices available to us.

Our exploration of the different lenses through which we can choose to interpret our reality, past and present, leads us to understand that our old mindsets constitute inner blocks to achieving the collective future we want. We each have an important role to play in creating a new collective reality by replacing our outworn, obsolete, and destructive mindsets with empowering new ones. Moreover, the choices we make as individuals and societies matter; in an interconnected world, each choice has an impact on everyone else. So we begin our quest for peace by understanding the dynamics of shifting our individual perceptions, thoughts, and feelings, resulting in positive collective energy and action.

To the extent that our interpretations lead us to believe that we are out of control and at the mercy of external events or to feel self-righteous and angry, the range of choices we see is very limited. This is because in these situations we feel like we are spinning our wheels and trapped in a cycle of negative emotions, largely characterized by fear, anxiety, helplesses, and depression. By contrast, any time we choose to interpret our reality by seeing and accepting it as it is without judgment, fully taking responsibility for our part in a situation, and developing the goal of finding opportunities for us and others that are latent in the challenges before us, we see that we have a much broader array of options. We then find ourselves in a position to choose our reactions to meet the challenge of the moment. The mere fact of feeling that we have options, and therefore room to maneuver and exercise agency in shaping our individual and collective lives causes our energy to shift from apathy and lethargy to motivation and determined drive. This ability to see the full range of options before us and to then take empowering action is exactly what humanity needs at this stage in its collective development as it faces systemic threats like climate change, global pandemics, and the risk of nuclear war.

Adjusting our mindset is therefore the foundational step we need to bring about lasting change. We must change our inner reality before we start to see changes in our outer reality. This seems to be one of those principles of life that operates in our individual and collective lives whether we acknowledge it or not. A simple example comes to mind.

Most of us have experienced times in our lives when our bodies have demonstrated outer evidences of poor health: our skin may be covered in spots, we may have accumulated extra pounds, our joints may ache, or we may simply feel lethargic. Although we can try for quick fixes like facial washes, crash diets, or caffeine, we know from experience that these measures are superficial and do not fix the root problem. Ultimately we find that the only solution is to change our lifestyle—to eat fresh fruits, vegetables, and grains; to substitute drinking caffeine with pure water; to get enough sleep and exercise; and to engage in mindfulness practice to better manage our stress.

Once we become aware that we have a broader range of choices than we initially thought, the next crucial step is to harness our gift of free will to pick an empowering choice and follow through on applying it. Until we do so, our options remain in the realm of potentiality and never become reality.

One of the most powerful yet least acknowledged truths is that at any given moment we have a choice to change who we are as individuals and as a society in order to create a better future and actualize our collective potential as an indivisible global community. Who we are today, individually or collectively, is a result of choices we have made about what to believe, how to behave, and how to react to our circumstances, all of which make up the sum of the experiences we have had to date. Who we are as individuals and a collective humanity today is merely a snapshot in time and does not serve as a predictor of who we can be tomorrow, nor of the social reality we can create. However, in order to effectively make more constructive choices, it is crucial that we first become aware of our past, and of the choices we have made about what we believe and how we behave.

Recognizing the mindsets and behavioral patterns that have brought us to where we are is a critical first step. It is only when we are clear-eyed about our past choices and have accepted full responsibility for decisions and choices that have led us to our current reality without judging ourselves, that we are capable of seeing and exploring alternative options of new perspectives and habits. This ability to see new possibilities and options is incredibly freeing.

Indeed, in his book *Man's Search for Meaning*, the famous psychiatrist and Holocaust survivor, Viktor Frankl described the power of free will as a "spiritual freedom" that was ultimately the measure of our independence of mind.[34] The gift of being able to exercise this power was, in his view, what allowed us to live lives of meaning and purpose. He repeatedly reiterated that while we might be stripped of almost everything we possess—from material belongings, to freedom of movement, speech or expression, to our very dignity—at the end of the day, the one property that nothing could take away was our ability to choose our reactions to circumstances. He commented that he had seen this phenomenon first-hand in his experiences in the Nazi concentration camps where he was held. He observed that while all of his fellow-inmates were subject to the same atrocities, there were stark differences in the way they chose to react. "In this living laboratory and on this testing ground, we watched and witnessed some of our comrades behave like swine while others behaved like saints," Frankl wrote. "Man has both potentialities within himself; which one is actualized depends on decisions but not on conditions."[35]

As we face the coronavirus pandemic, we observe and experience the full range of choices and reactions that people and nations are making in straitened circumstances. Some are trapped in a self-made snare of limiting beliefs that drives them to put the interests of their nations first by attempting to hoard access to critical resources like personal protective gear, ventilators, and vaccines, while others are breaking out of the outworn notions that their nation can handle the pandemic alone and are choosing instead to collaborate, coordinate, and share these same resources with other nations and people.

Shawn Achor sheds light on the most effective way we can exercise the power of choice. As we discussed above, in his book *The Happiness Advantage*, Achor comments that the typical human tendency that arises when we are faced with a challenge is to repeat the same behavior that generated the challenge, thus getting the same negative results and making no progress. He characterizes this tendency as the "first path," or first category of choice. Alternatively, we take the "second path," where we take a few steps back, undoing strides we have made toward progress and achieving even worse outcomes. Ultimately, Achor suggests that the key to happiness and success actually lies in opting for a "third path" that requires using the momentum born of our plunge toward disaster and failure to catapult ourselves in a new direction that we have never before considered. It is this ability to be creative especially in times of difficulty, see new options, and exercise our free will in new ways that gets us out of the morass in which we find ourselves and leads to a quantum leap in growth. It is this kind of choice that determines whether tests we encounter become stumbling blocks or serve as stepping-stones towards further growth.[36]

An example that immediately leaps to mind in considering Achor's work is Europe's experience with Brexit. Britain's decision to leave the European Union in 2017 was met with dismay and predictions of economic and other disasters. It was interesting to observe that the reaction of many countries in Europe was to continue with the same policies and patterns that had alienated Britain from the European Union in the first place, instead of undertaking reforms to reel Britain back. It was similarly eye-opening to see that some countries, such as Poland, called for taking steps that would result in reclaiming greater autonomy for E.U. member states, giving them more freedom from the authority of Brussels over their internal affairs, thereby undoing the hard-won progress in the direction of deeper European integration.

What was heartening, however, was to hear, amid alarmist and pessimistic messages, certain positive voices calling for Europe to take a third path toward collective growth marked by deeper integration. These voices could be heard very clearly in a ground-breaking report produced by the foreign ministers of France and Germany at the time, Jean-Marc Ayrault and Frank-Walter Steinmeier.[37]

In this report they acknowledged that Europe was in the crucible of a severe test from which they were confident it would emerge stronger than ever. They viewed the crisis caused by Brexit as an opportunity to develop common answers to their common challenges. Consequently, they called for closer cooperation on matters relating to defense, security, and intelligence-sharing; the joint patrolling of external borders; a common migration and asylum policy; harmonization of corporation tax; and other financial reforms. They were so positive in their outlook that they went so far as to confidently predict that the countries of the E.U. would move further toward political integration and union. Although Britain ultimately opted not to remain in the European Union and instead pushed forward toward a tumultuous departure in 2020, the remaining 27 members of the union still have the option of working toward a more deeply integrated E.U. through reforming certain key areas. There is also always the possibility that if such reforms were to take place, Britain might wish to rejoin a stronger, better E.U. at some point in the future.

Finding a third way to respond to the global challenges facing us, from the current pandemic to the slower-moving and colossal threat of climate change, is the vital opportunity before us. In case we missed it before, it is now becoming blindingly obvious that all nations are bound together as one. We all sink or swim together. The advantage of one nation can only be ensured by guaranteeing the advantage of all nations.

Just as each of us is born with inherent capacity and potential that can only be actualized through exercising our power of volition, so, too, our capacity to create a better world depends on the choices we make as a global society. Moreover, the two are often interrelated, especially when it comes to choices made by people who are in positions of influence or power. A striking example of this truth lies in South Africa's experience with Nelson and Winnie Mandela. Both husband and wife suffered tremendously because of the injustices of the apartheid system in South Africa. Yet, the ways in which they ultimately chose to view their suffering and respond to it could not have been more different, with starkly divergent consequences for South African people.

Nelson Mandela started his activism through peaceful protest and acts of civil disobedience against unjust laws. He quickly realized that this method was insufficient to get rid of the violent and racist system of apartheid, so he created the paramilitary arm of the African National Congress. He was subsequently imprisoned for 27 years for planning bomb attacks. Rather than letting his anger at his continued oppression fester, Mandela spent his years in prison preparing himself for a time when he would emerge and lead his people to freedom. Despite the degree of injustice and harm perpetrated against him, his greatest focus during that time was to change himself. Mandela entered prison for acts of violence born of a vengeful mindset. By the time of his release, he had transformed his vision into a reconciliatory one. As he famously said after his release, "Resentment is like drinking poison and then hoping it will kill your enemies."[38]

In the end, he was able to unify the South African people in a nonracial democracy and avoid a bloody civil war. At his inauguration as South Africa's first Black president, Mandela declared, "The time for the healing of the wounds has come. The moment to bridge the chasms that divide us has come. The time to build is upon us."[39]

By contrast, his wife Winnie always hated her white oppressors and chose to react to their oppression with a deliberate use of violence. She was found to have instigated a reign of terror and to have been accountable for gross violations of human rights committed by her security detail. She famously endorsed the practice of "necklacing," which was a form of summary execution meted out to people suspected of being collaborators of the apartheid government or police informers, and thus traitors to the cause of Black liberation. This technique consisted of hanging rubber tires around the necks of the suspected traitors, filling them with gasoline, and setting them alight.

Winnie's violent tactics caused far more pain and destruction than justice and healing. Although she and her husband faced similar injustices, Winnie chose to respond to her oppression with extreme violence and hatred, while Nelson chose unity, forgiveness, and reconciliation. As Thomas Hibbs points out, "unlike many of his colleagues, and especially unlike Winnie, Nelson never [became] addicted to violence or vengeance."[40] Nelson's divergent approach and his choice to renounce violence ultimately spared thousands of lives and led to unprecedented reconciliation and healing.

The COVID-19 pandemic has also served as a universal crash course in understanding how our daily choices at the individual and collective levels shape our future and create our reality. A recent study conducted at Columbia University shows that if the United States had imposed social distancing requirements just one week earlier than it did, as many as 36,000 lives would have been saved. Had these requirements been imposed two weeks earlier we would have had 83 percent fewer deaths.[41] By wearing masks when we go outside we protect others from illness or even death, especially in view of the fact that up to 45 percent of COVID-19 cases may be asymptomatic.[42] It is clear, therefore, that even seemingly mundane choices about how we behave can have massive effects on our communities. Whether we are sensible about social distancing and wearing masks can tangibly mark the difference between large-scale life or death and the collapse or survival of our health-care systems. These choices will also impact the overall health of our economy, as they will determine how long we must lock down our businesses in order to reduce community spread of the virus. Experience has already demonstrated that countries that imposed and acceded to these requirements early have been able to contain the virus to a level where they have been able to open up their economies.

Our challenge, then, is first to envision the world we want, the future we deserve, and the kind of human beings we want to be, and then to bend our collective will with tenacious determination and ceaseless effort to achieve these goals.

The key to tackling this challenge is to start becoming conscious of the way we tend to interpret events and reality, and make the necessary shifts in our mindset to allow for growth. As we saw earlier, a profound shift in emotion and energy is possible when we change our mindset about who we are as human beings, what our history represents, and the trials that our global community is currently facing. Rather than viewing ourselves as evil in nature, seeing our history as a demonstration that we are incorrigibly violent and selfish, and experiencing our present crises as helpless victims, we put our behavior and its resulting circumstances in the context of our evolution through stages of collective growth toward maturity. We accept responsibility for the choices we have made that have created our current circumstances and commit ourselves to make different, more constructive ones. After recognizing the hope and potential latent in ourselves and this historic moment, our altered perspective shifts us from a state in which we feel helpless and paralyzed to a state of hope, energy, and determination where we see in front of us a broad array of choices with which to address the obstacles before us.

Chapter 5

Shifting Our Collective
Mindsets and Habits

OLD MINDSET 4: GLOBALIZATION IS TO
BLAME FOR OUR TROUBLES

One of the dominant mindsets about our current global situation is the widespread belief that globalization is the cause of many international problems. A core feeling at the root of this belief is the fear of losing national autonomy and becoming reliant on other states—globalization leads to interdependence, which necessitates a decrease in national independence. This discomfort with thinking we need other nations leads us to believe globalization is making us weaker. The corollary of this mentality is that we need to get back the power that we have given away—namely national sovereignty. Instinctively, we move to more insular practices in the name of independence and autonomy.

We also blame globalization for increases in inequality, cultural homogeneity, and environmental devastation. With the advent of global commerce, generic North American brands like Starbucks and McDonald's can be found in seemingly every corner of the globe; globalization is stripping away the unique cultures of peoples and nations. Increased international trade is creating vast wealth gaps, and multinational corporations operate with unregulated political power, exploiting workers and resources. Easy international travel is generating unprecedented immigration, which is often seen as a threat to jobs and other opportunities for a nation's citizens. Outsourcing workers from other countries is causing the deindustrialization of developed countries and contributing to the exploitation of workers in developing countries. And, as our recent experience with COVID-19 is demonstrating, globalization makes it easier for diseases to spread rapidly on an unbounded global scale.

OLD HABITS OF ISOLATIONISM, XENOPHOBIA, TRIBALISM AND POLARIZATION

As we begin to identify and examine our maladaptive collective habits we will find that they sometimes appear in clusters because they have sprung from and are rooted in a common disempowering interpretation of our social reality. We can understand this clustering phenomenon by considering the human body. When the immune system is taxed in a sustained manner for long periods of time it can become reactive and prone to autoimmune diseases. What is interesting is that once a person develops one autoimmune disease their chances of developing others is significantly greater.[43] The same pattern is true of the single organism of our global community. To the extent that we harbor dysfunctional habits that have grown out of the soil of our destructive mindsets, weakening our immune system and making it reactive, we have become susceptible to spawning new dysfunctional habits.

For example, the habits of isolationism, xenophobia, tribalism and polarization, and nationalism are closely interrelated and rooted in the destructive mindset that the interests of different groups of human beings—whether categorized by race, ethnicity, or national identity—are at odds with each other. Let's examine and break down each of these habits.

Isolationism

The first of these widespread and damaging behaviors is isolationism. This work defines isolationism as the habit of remaining aloof from the affairs or interests of other groups, especially the political affairs of other countries. It is an act of turning inward as a group or nation, hunkering down, and focusing on taking care of one's isolated interests. It is based on a fundamental misunderstanding that, particularly in times of difficulty for ourselves or for others, we are better off letting each group or nation handle its own challenges. In that sense it is an abdication of responsibility to assist others or to call on others to assist us in times of need. While such a habit might make sense in a world in which each nation is self-sufficient and completely independent of its sister nations, in today's world of intense interconnectedness and interdependence it makes no sense. Indeed, it is counterproductive.

A prime example of the destructiveness of isolationism is the way the international community chose to respond to the unfolding crises in Syria starting in 2011. Despite clear evidence that chemical weapons were being used against the people of Syria and despite the country's rapid descent into civil war between the government and militia groups, the international community was content to sit back and do nothing. It justified its inaction on the grounds that this was an internal problem for the Syrians to solve on their own. Meanwhile, at least 400,000 Syrians died and 6.2 million have been internally displaced.[44] As the disintegration intensified it spawned several new problems that extended beyond the borders of Syria, creating malaise in countries both in the region and beyond. One of the problems was that 5.6 million Syrians fled the country as refugees and sought refuge in neighboring countries including Jordan, Lebanon, and Turkey. Their presence imposed both economic and social pressures in those countries. As time went on large numbers of refugees attempted to seek safety in Europe. In turn, European countries responded with strong backlash against the migrants, leaning into feelings of xenophobia and nationalism. As a result, European countries closed their borders, right-wing parties maximized the xenophobic rhetoric to gain ascendancy, and disunity arose within the European Union. The refugee crisis was not the only fallout of the Syrian conflict that was felt by the international community. The conflict created a fertile environment for the rise and training of a new generation of terrorists, such as the group known as the Islamic State in Iraq and the Levant (ISIL), whose goal was to create a new Islamic state in Iraq and Syria, and that demonstrated its propensity for committing acts of brutal violence against Sunnis, Shiites, and foreigners alike as a means of achieving its ends. Despite the growing horrors of the Syrian conflict both inside and outside Syria, the international community found itself impotent to end the violence and suffering. By the time the international community realized that Syria's supposedly internal problem was affecting the entire region, and indeed the world, it was too late. Despite attempts to impose effective sanctions on Syria, the U.N. Security Council found itself impotent to do so because Russia vetoed proposed resolutions on at least three different occasions. At some point the conflict had drawn so many countries into the fray on opposing sides that it was being described in some quarters as a "proto world war."[45]

Another way in which we have seen the habit of isolationism play out is through the fragmentation it has caused. As our turbulent adolescent world acts out, creating ever-increasing global challenges and struggling to solve them, we see the troubling phenomenon of isolationism that gives rise to fragmentation with greater frequency in many parts of the world. Reacting to the local effects of these global challenges and dissatisfied with responses by their national political unions, many people clamor for political independence and self-determination. They want to separate from their states, believing that it will afford them more control over their destinies and will preserve them from going down with the sinking ships of their larger communities. This belief is what animates the Kurds to want autonomy within both Turkey and Iraq. It is what drove the citizens of Crimea to secede from Ukraine, the people of South Sudan to secede from Sudan and create their own independent state in 2011, and the people of Eritrea to separate from Ethiopia to create a country of their own in 1993. It is the same drive that has led the residents of Hong Kong to engage in large-scale and sustained protests asking for the freedom to elect their own government without interference by central authority in Beijing, and enabled the Catalans to gain independence from Spain. Brexit is another prime example of this move towards isolationism, separatism, and fragmentation. The citizens of Britain fought bitterly to withdraw from the European Union, believing that the economic malaise of their country was due to the free movement of people, and wishing to retake control of their destiny by breaking free of the dictates imposed by Brussels. The break-up has led to severe polarization and disunity within Britain. Moreover, this separation does not solve some key collective problems like climate change, terrorism, security, or the strength of the economy.

Indeed, separation not only fails to solve the problems, but it is actively harmful. On the one hand, causing communities to fragment into smaller and smaller units leads to disunity and strife among peoples and nations, which exacerbates problems or even creates new ones. On the other hand, the move toward separatism and isolation fails to take into account the fact of our interdependence—the global nature of these crises demands global solutions that cannot be found when humanity is more fragmented. Continuing along this path will reverse much of the progress that humanity has made in creating concentric circles of loyalty and integration that are entirely compatible with each other. Pursuing this course of action will only lead us backward and return us to its logical conclusion: tribalism. It is imperative, therefore, that we redouble our efforts to reverse course and put humanity back on the path of increased integration and support rather than fragmentation.

Xenophobia

Like our habit of isolationism, xenophobia grows out of a mindset that perceives the superficial differences between human beings as reasons to rank them as being better or worse than one another. Consequently, it breeds suspicion, fear, and ignorance of the "other" and creates a mental construct that ensures that the "other" remains separate. In doing so, it completely disregards the reality of the oneness of humankind and fails to use this principle to our advantage. The soil in which it flourishes is the antithesis of the mindset that recognizes that humanity is a single organism with fused interests. Yet the emotions that underlie xenophobia are more negatively charged than those that underlie isolationism—they involve feelings of active hatred, fear, or prejudice against people from other countries.

Perhaps the most notorious example of xenophobia in recent years has been the United States' anti-Mexican rhetoric and policies beginning in the early 20th century. Mexican workers had historically provided labor value to the U.S., crossing the border to work at factories at a relatively cheap cost. However, Americans' eagerness to recruit workers from across the border quickly dissolved into blame as the Great Depression caused widespread economic panic. Suddenly, Mexicans were a threat to job opportunities and security of American citizens. Mexicans were cast as racially inferior, savages, and menaces to the American way of life. Calls to "get rid of the Mexicans" grew so widespread that mass deportation of Mexicans from the U.S. became commonplace. Between 1929 to 1935 the federal government deported 82,400 Mexicans, a number representing almost 50 percent of all deportations, despite the fact that Mexicans made up only 1 percent of the U.S. population at the time.[46]

Over the next several decades, Mexicans continued to be targeted as racially inferior and socially and economically threatening to the American public. Common rhetoric categorized Mexicans as "illegal," and media and political references described Mexican immigration as "floods" and "waves," heightening the fear factor by criminalizing Mexicans and emphasizing how these immigrants would sweep away an American way of life. Anti-Mexican racism and xenophobia remains a strong American tradition today, with an administration that won the 2016 election on a platform largely constituting anti-Mexican xenophobia such as building a wall to keep out the neighboring Mexicans. In his presidential announcement speech in June 2016, President Trump announced, "When Mexico sends its people, they're not sending their best. ... They're sending people that have lots of problems, and they're bringing those problems with us. They're bringing drugs. They're bringing crime. They're rapists." Trump's successful presidential bid on a platform that called on Americans' long-held fear and racism toward Mexicans demonstrated clearly that the U.S. is still deeply enmeshed in xenophobic beliefs. As a result, recent years have seen an increase in inhumane treatment of immigrants at the U.S.-Mexico border, including but not limited to overcrowding at immigration detention centers, heartbreaking family separation at the border, and an increase in child deaths at the border.[47]

In Poland the far-right Law and Justice party that came into power at the height of the migrant crisis in 2015 was very vocal about its refusal to open its door to immigrants, and rejected the pleas of North African and Middle Eastern migrants fleeing persecution, hunger, and war in search of safety and opportunity. As a result, an overflow of migrants remained stuck in inhumane refugee camps in southern Europe, and experienced further hunger, separation, and strife. Yet, as time went on, it turned out that Poland was quietly accepting large numbers of migrant workers—beyond anything seen in its modern history—but only from similar ethnic and religious backgrounds, most of whom were Christians from Ukraine. Poland's extreme xenophobia and the mentality of "Poland for Poles"—rhetoric eerily similar to the Third Reich motto "Germany for Germans" and the Ku Klux Klan's "America for Americans"—directly contributed to mass human rights deprivations.[48]

Such prejudices manifest themselves in many more incredibly harmful actions and consequences as countries desperately seek to ensure separation between the members of their self-assigned national identity and others. However, the negative impacts of xenophobia are not limited to the groups targeted by this oppression; acts of xenophobia often also have detrimental effects on the states perpetrating them. A recent example that highlights the strange self-destructive nature of xenophobia is Italy. In spring 2019, Matteo Salvini's populist party argued that women's rights to abortion in Italy should be curtailed because they led to the reduction in the national birthrate. This decrease would supposedly then enhance the risk that the balance between Italians and other ethnic and religious groups might be upset, particularly as it related to Muslims from Africa.[49] Thus, prejudice against foreigners, and African Muslims in particular, led to undue hardships being imposed on Italian women, in addition to Islamophobic and anti-African prejudice.

Tribalism and Polarization

The third ubiquitous maladaptive habit that we observe arising out of our misguided perception that human beings and communities should function separately from one another is tribalism. The fundamental idea underlying tribalism is that we belong to a team and that our team is always right. Consequently, there is always a tinge of superiority, self-righteousness, entitlement, and willingness to blame another team for problems that arise.

One of the hallmarks of tribalism is the ever-present spirit of competition grounded in a mindset of scarcity. The combination of these two elements makes those engaged in tribalism very prone to conflict. It also makes them reluctant to abide by a set of rules that apply equally to everyone.

The most obvious manifestation of this habit is in the system of partisan politics. So many nations are divided by political parties who, by their very nature, stand in opposition to one another, each believing that they are right and have exclusive access to "the truth" as they see it. Consequently, harsh political battles ensue and generate extreme polarization among people, even within one national identity. The United States' bipartisan system is a prime example of this polarization. We need look no further than the recent 2016 election, which drove even deeper a longstanding wedge between the two parties. The conviction of the two dominant parties in the rightness of their views and policies and the bitterness held by members of opposing parties have torn apart families, communities, and the entire nation. It is no wonder that in his famous farewell address in 1796, President George Washington warned that political parties, while occasionally achieving certain popular ends, would lead to the infant nation's demise. Washington said:

> "However [political parties] may now and then answer popular ends, they are likely in the course of time and things to become potent engines, by

which cunning, ambitious, and unprincipled men will be enabled to subvert the power of the people and to usurp for themselves the reigns of government, destroying afterwards the very engines which have lifted them to unjust dominion."[50]

We have seen his warning play out in the United States. When we most needed to be unified and strong in order to withstand the crisis of the COVID-19 pandemic and the economic recession it brought in its wake, our social immune system had already been severely compromised by partisan rivalry and division, weakening our capacity to act in unity to overcome the challenge.

One of the strange characteristics of polarization is that people take sides and fight hard for an entrenched position based on fear and mistrust of the opposing party, and yet when they get the power they so desire they have no constructive ideas. An example of this phenomenon is the French Yellow Vest movement that began in late 2018. Initially, protesters took to the streets demanding for Macron to repeal a new fuel tax hike and reduce the recent surge in diesel prices. However, as protests went on, the specifics of what they wanted dissolved from a singular purpose to encapsulate an amorphous set of demands driven by a generalized sense of economic injustice and anti-establishment sentiment, without a proposal of what positive actions should be taken instead.[51]

Similarly, the movement for Brexit was driven by a strong desire to leave the European Union, take back control of legislation and regulation, and restrict migration without creating a plan to deal with the economic and political impacts of leaving the union. Likewise, while there were strong moves along party lines in the U.S. to scrap the Affordable Care Act in 2017, very little thought was given to what would replace it.

OLD HABIT OF NATIONALISM

One of the most baneful and destructive habits we have cultivated is nationalism. While identifying with our own nation and ardently supporting its interests can inspire us to exert our energies toward advancing the fields of education, scientific discovery, and music and arts—all of which are laudable and essentially amount to a healthy and intelligent patriotism—nationalism by contrast is destructive. What makes nationalism so pernicious is that one seeks to advance the interests of one's own nation, particularly at the expense of others, in the mistaken belief that to survive and thrive nations must remain in perpetual competition with each other with some winning and others losing. This feature of nationalism results in tremendous disadvantage both to the nation involved and to the entire world.

Historically, extreme examples of nationalism include the aggressive expansion, exploitation, and mass murders associated with fascist governments in the mid 1900s. More recently emerging cases include the new wave of nationalism across much of Western Europe and the U.S., reflected in slogans like "Make America Great Again," and in Britain, "Take Back Control" from the European Union.[52] However, nationalism rears its ugly head even in the absence of extreme ideologies like fascism. A good example is the competition to access critical, limited natural resources like fresh water. One case study is the massive dam that Ethiopia started building on the Blue Nile in 2011. Its two prime purposes in building the dam were to provide electricity for more than half of Ethiopia's citizens who do not have access to it, and to thereby pull them out of poverty. Yet, its neighbors, Egypt and Sudan, have been worried about the extent to which the filling and operation of the dam will reduce what they consider to be their rightful share to the Nile waters on which they so heavily depend. Egypt is especially concerned as it relies more heavily on the Nile for irrigation and drinking water than the other 10 countries that share its basin, with 90 percent of Egypt's 100 million citizens living on the Nile's banks.[53] It argues, based on its own internal estimates, that it will lose 200,000 acres of agricultural land for every reduction of 1 billion cubic meters of water, resulting in a loss of livelihood for 1 million inhabitants.[54]

It is particularly worried that the rate at which Ethiopia fills the 74 billion cubic meters of reservoir, currently proposed to take three to four years, will reduce the water that accumulates and is available to it in Lake Nasser, Egypt's own massive reservoir on the Nile, especially in times of drought. It has therefore asked Ethiopia to reduce the rate of filling by drawing it out to somewhere between nine and twelve years, but the two countries have yet to reach an agreement on this and a number of other technical and legal matters relating to the operation of the dam.

Both Sudan and Egypt have legitimate needs that they are seeking to satisfy by locking up rights to use the Nile's waters. Their concerns were exacerbated when Ethiopia took the unilateral decision to begin filling the reservoir—which is roughly the size of London—starting in July 2020, before the three countries were able to conclude their multi-year negotiations and arrive at an agreement about how the dam would be filled and operated.[55] Ultimately, the only way to meet these needs without conflict is through collaboration, including a plan to coordinate the operation of the Egyptian and Ethiopian dams respectively to ensure that they can both be filled in a manner that is equitable, rather than resorting to a competitive, nationalistic approach.

In a world that is as interconnected and interdependent as ours it is impossible for any nation to survive and thrive on its own, especially at the expense of other nations. Returning to the analogy of the world as the human body, it makes no sense for the liver to say to the kidneys, "I don't care if you have cancer. I am focused exclusively on my own health, regardless of what happens to you." Just as these organs, albeit different in function and capacity, are part of one single body, so too, each nation, although different in customs, outlooks, and habits, is a part of the global body politic. If one nation is ailing, the effect will eventually be felt by all, and the well-being of any one nation is dependent upon the well-being of the global community.

The corrosive effects of nationalism can best be understood by exploring its effect on our collective ability to effectively respond to some of our most intractable global challenges.

COVID-19

Never has the world so tangibly experienced the consequences of its interconnectedness as it has in its fight against the COVID-19 pandemic. With every passing day it becomes clearer that decisions one country makes about how to contain the virus have direct effects on other countries around the world. Such decisions range from whether borders are closed or left open, whether information about the spread of the virus is shared openly or kept hidden, whether countries invest in the production and procurement of personal protective equipment to protect their health workers and their population, whether nations implement rules regarding social distancing and wearing masks, and so on. Decisions about whether to allow flights and movement between countries or prevent them is greatly impacting tourism, which in turn affects many countries with tourism-based economies. The ability to harvest crops in many countries is affected when migrant workers who play a key role in this activity are barred from entering a country, leading to economic devastation for farmers, as well as nationwide food shortages. The ability to manufacture goods ranging from small electronic equipment to automobiles is affected by disruptions in global supply chains when various countries halt production because of the virus. The list goes on. As time passes by it becomes increasingly apparent that in order to effectively contain the virus and restart the global economy, all nations must learn to consult, cooperate, and collaborate to make decisions that affect their collective future.

The Financial Crises of the 2000s

The COVID-19 pandemic is not the first opportunity that humanity has had to learn that the time for nationalism has come and gone. During both the U.S. financial crisis of 2007–2009 and the European debt crisis of 2010-2012, countries began to understand that their financial destiny was inextricably woven with that of others. Although the causes of the 2007 financial crisis were largely internal to the U.S., the impacts were far-reaching. When the housing bubble burst in the U.S. in 2007, several financial institutions, most notably Lehman Brothers, collapsed. Because of the interconnectedness of the U.S. financial system with the world's financial systems, many were concerned about the risk of contagion that would result in other banks around the world collapsing. To forestall such a domino effect, the U.S. government stepped in with massive bailouts and government takeovers of other financial institutions. Despite its actions, the 2008 financial crisis pushed other global financial systems close to collapse.

One of the effects of the U.S. financial crisis was that the global economy slowed down. This in turn led to reduced tax revenues and exposed unsustainable fiscal policies in certain European countries, as well as many others around the globe. In Europe, reduced tax revenues meant that a number of countries struggled to pay back debts they had accumulated over decades. These countries included Greece, Portugal, Spain, Italy, and Ireland. As the extent of the Greek budget deficit became known, investors demanded higher yields on Greece's bonds to compensate them for the additional risks they were taking by investing in the Greek economy, exacerbating the country's debt and ultimately requiring a number of bailouts by the European Union and the International Monetary Fund. Ireland and Portugal also had to be bailed out.

During these fraught years, financial and political leaders in countries like the United States and China acknowledged the reality of their interconnectedness when they expressed anxiety about the effect of the growing European crisis on their economic well-being, and the threat of a world-wide recession. World leaders sounded warnings both privately and in public that Europe's problems were dragging their nations down, too. News media echoed these concerns and their roots in world-wide interconnectivity. Thus *The Economist* bluntly stated, "it is not just the euro that is at risk, but the future of the European Union and the health of the world economy."[56] Nations worried that another collapse of the financial system like the one precipitated in 2008 would reverberate around the world, dooming Europe, the United States, and emerging countries to a prolonged downturn, or worse. In an effort to protect itself from such an impact, the United States sent Secretary of the Treasury Timothy Geithner to Europe on more than one occasion to dispense advice on the sovereign-debt crisis. His main goal was to press for decisive European action for the good of the global economy.[57]

Flaws in the Nuclear Non-Proliferation Treaty

Another area in which nationalism has played a destructive role in making the world less peaceful and secure involves the international system established to prevent the proliferation of nuclear weapons. In 1970 the international Treaty on the Non-Proliferation of Nuclear Weapons (NPT) came into force. Its main aim was to ensure that civilian nuclear material would not be diverted for military purposes. Despite its initial success, over time certain fundamental weaknesses in the system it established became apparent and now threaten to undermine the entire project. The International Atomic Energy Agency (IAEA), created in 1957 to promote the peaceful use of atomic energy under a system of international safeguards, was designated to serve as the primary mechanism for ensuring compliance with the NPT. However, the IAEA has been only partially successful in achieving its mandate and it needs to be considerably strengthened if the world community is serious about stemming the tide of nuclear proliferation. It is worth taking a closer look at how weaknesses in the NPT and the limited success of the IAEA—that have resulted in the near collapse of the system designed to safeguard us from the threat of nuclear destruction—stem from our collective habit of nationalism and its corollary, the unwillingness of nations to cede a modicum of sovereignty to ensure international peace and security.

The first fundamental flaw in the NPT system is that states are free to choose whether they will sign on as a party to the treaty or not. Given that the treaty is so pivotal to maintaining peace and keeping our world safe, participation should be mandatory. Given the unprecedented dangers posed by nuclear weapons of mass destruction to the safety, peace, security, and the very existence of the peoples of the world, the international community must absolutely demand that all of its member states be required to adhere to the NPT. This is an area in which national sovereignty must be curtailed for the good of the world community.

The second flaw is a corollary to the first. The NPT allows for a state party to withdraw, with minimal conditions for withdrawal and only a brief period of advance notice required. For example, a member state may withdraw from the NPT on a mere three months' notice to the other parties and to the U.N. Security Council. It may do so "if it decides that extraordinary events, related to the subject matter of this Treaty, have jeopardized the supreme interest of its country." In addition, withdrawal carries with it no consequences, even if the state is found to have been in breach of its obligations prior to its departure. It defies belief, given the dangers to our peace and security posed by weapons of mass destruction, that we would even entertain the notion of allowing a state party to this treaty, so fundamental to the peace of the world, to withdraw from it in the first place. But then facilitating exit by allowing withdrawal to be based solely on a state's own decision justified on the basis of "extraordinary events"—a term left undefined in the treaty—in the name of honoring state sovereignty ensures that the NPT will unravel. A treaty of this immensity should be binding for all states without exception, and with no option for withdrawal.

The third fundamental flaw in the NPT is the absence of a reliable and shared system of intelligence, coupled with robust monitoring and verification to ensure that states that have agreed to it actually comply with their obligations. The NPT does have a system of international safeguards in place to ensure that its provisions are obeyed. The aim is to prevent nuclear energy from being diverted from peaceful uses to nuclear weapons or explosive devices. These safeguards are embodied in agreements that are negotiated between the IAEA and states party to the NPT. The IAEA's role is to serve as the world's international inspectorate, verifying that the safeguards are adhered to. However, over time it has become apparent that both the safeguards and the scope of the IAEA's authority have been inadequate to bring violations of the NPT to the attention of the international community in a timely manner. For example, the IAEA's inspectors had to give advance notice that they were planning to investigate the country whose nuclear facilities they wanted to inspect. Such notice allowed the country to hide the materials in other locations before the arrival of the inspectors, thwarting their mission. Even after the U.N. Special Commission was created to find evidence of an illicit nuclear program in Iraq and given broad powers of unrestricted movement in Iraq without needing to give advance notice, the Iraqis engaged in cat and mouse games with UNSCOM inspectors. Television footage in the summer of 1991 showed inspectors arriving through the front door of buildings they were supposed to inspect while materials were simultaneously being pulled out of the building and loaded into trucks that were filmed driving away. The notice requirement was put into place because nations were more interested in safeguarding their narrow national self-interest than serving the interests of the global community.

Another example of nationalism at work in the context of IAEA inspections was that inspectors were limited in the geographic scope of their investigations. The country in question could limit the inspections to certain sites, buildings, and even rooms within a building on the justification that their national security demanded it. It was due to these severe constraints—driven by nationalism—on the ability of the IAEA to effectively monitor countries' nuclear activities that the international community failed to detect Iran's undeclared nuclear activities and only learned about them from dissidents and not as a result of the safeguards system. Similarly, the world only learned about North Korea's nuclear activities when North Korea itself decided to divulge its secret. Unsurprisingly, North Korea then proceeded to withdraw from the NPT. Finally, we learned about Iraq's clandestine pursuit of a program to develop nuclear weapons after the Persian Gulf War in 1991, not because of the efficacy of the safeguards system.

As a result of these clear failures, the IAEA set up a new program to monitor and verify compliance with the NPT provisions prohibiting diversion of declared nuclear materials and to increase its capability to detect secret nuclear programs.[58] Unfortunately, the new program suffers from its own inadequacies and limitations, which again result from excessively clinging to national sovereignty. One example of such an inadequacy is the national security exception that allows a member state, through its sole discretion, to exclude the application of the new rules on the grounds that they have national security implications. A state that is secretly developing nuclear weapons could easily rely on this exclusion to hide such activities from the IAEA.[59]

What we have seen is an example of the pernicious effects of nationalism in an area as crucial to international life as our safety from nuclear war. Nuclear weapons pose a severe threat to the security of the human race as a whole, yet our insistence on clinging to our old habit of nationalism exacerbates this threat and has hindered our ability to craft an international system of monitoring and inspections that guarantees our collective protection against the scourge of these weapons. Even as the international community has found itself impotent to tackle existing challenges of nuclear proliferation manifested in the illicit nuclear proliferation programs of North Korea and Iran, it finds itself confronted with the possibility of new threats on this front. American intelligence agencies believe that Saudi Arabia, with China's help, may be in the process of building capacities to produce nuclear fuel.[60]

Climate Change

Climate change is another global challenge that has repeatedly exposed the harm of nationalism. After the pandemic, it is likely the biggest danger the world currently faces. It touches every aspect of life on this planet, affecting not only our environment, health, and physical well-being, but our security as well, as it has the potential to cause massive, globally destabilizing conflict. We have long known that carbon dioxide traps heat at the surface of the planet. The more carbon dioxide we emit, the higher the earth's temperature becomes. The rise in the earth's temperature is melting the world's glaciers, ice sheets, and snow caps at unprecedented rates. Melting, in turn, is causing the oceans to rise rapidly, and they will eventually submerge large swathes of heavily populated coastal areas and entire island nations. The unexpectedly rapid rate at which glaciers in Greenland alone are melting is predicted to raise sea levels up to 67 centimeters by the end of this century and to cause 400 million people worldwide to be affected by coastal flooding.[61] Indeed, scientists underscore that the historical record teaches us that when the earth's temperature rises even by a few degrees, waters rise by as much as several hundred feet. What is alarming is that when carbon dioxide levels have risen naturally in the distant past, this shift happened over many tens and hundreds of thousands of years, giving life time to adapt. Now it is occurring with unprecedented rapidity—within a few hundred years—because of how quickly humans are releasing carbon dioxide into the atmosphere.

Global warming is also projected to cause more floods, storms, droughts, and heat waves, and eventually to expand and create new deserts. The combination of losing large coastal areas and the desertification of other areas will result in a dwindling amount of land available to grow food, obtain water, and house a rapidly growing global population, straining our agriculture and disrupting our economies. In short, we will experience worse storms, more flash floods, and more enduring droughts that lead to wide-spread wildfires. As a result, many plants and animals on land and water will become extinct. While many people were skeptical, thinking that these projections and warnings were exaggerated, recent repeated experiences are demonstrating that the impact of climate change is occuring more quickly than we had imagined, and at an accelerated pace.

We need look no further than the worldwide experiences with massive wildfires in 2019 and 2020. In Australia a prolonged period of drought has led to wildfires that start as much as three months earlier than usual, occur more frequently, are more intense, and last longer. These fires have destroyed human lives and property and have razed more than 104,000 square kilometers of rainforests and parkland. It is estimated that they have decimated more than a billion animals, threatening to put many species into extinction. Plants and habitats necessary for surviving animals to find food and shelter have also been destroyed.[62] One of the knock-on effects of these fires and others around the world is that large amounts of ash and debris end up in rivers and streams, severely reducing the amount of dissolved oxygen in those ecosystems and killing fish and other forms of life. The ash and debris has also polluted drinking water supplies, making them unsafe for human consumption.[63] Wildfires caused by climate change have by no means been limited to Australia. They have become a global phenomenon, from California and Canada to Greece and Portugal.[64]

They had a devastating impact on the West Coast of the United States during the summer of 2020. Over one million acres burned in the state of Oregon alone, while in California more than three million burned. Hundreds of thousands of people have been forced from their homes, and entire communities have been lost. It is becoming increasingly evident that while some of the devastation can be attributed to mismanagement of forests, much of it is due to climate change, which has led to long periods of drought and heat waves that have turned large swathes of forest into tinder.[65] Moreover, there has been an unprecedented number of lightning strikes—12,000 over the course of a single weekend—that reportedly started many of the 585 fires across the state of California and made it more dangerous for firefighters to work.[66]

Even more concerning is the fact that rainforests that are regarded as lungs for the entire world, absorbing vast quantities of carbon dioxide and acting as vast carbon storehouses while producing much-needed oxygen in return, are being destroyed at an unprecedented pace. These include the Amazon rainforest, where massive fires have burnt vast tracts of the forest. As the trees burn, not only do we lose their capacity to absorb large quantities of carbon dioxide, but worse still, they release vast amounts of trapped carbon dioxide back into the atmosphere, exacerbating global warming.[67]

As though the forest fires in the Amazon were not damaging enough, the rainforest in the Congo Basin, which is the second largest rainforest in the world after the Amazon, and is regarded as the world's "second lung" is also in danger of burning.[68] All the way at the other end of the world, massive wildfires decimated seven million acres of land in Siberia in 2019. As a result of an unusually warm winter due to climate change, the wildfires started again in Siberia in the spring of 2020, at which point they were already between three to ten times bigger than they were the previous year. Scientists have concluded with high confidence that the unprecedented heat wave in the first six months of 2020 is attributable to global warming, which has made the high temperatures 600 times more likely.[69] In addition to the fires, the rise in temperatures is melting permafrost, releasing vast amounts of carbon dioxide stored in it and further exacerbating climate change.[70]

With input from a wide range of scientists, the United Nations Intergovernmental Panel on Climate Change (IPCC), a U.N. body established by the United Nations Environment Program and the World Meteorological Organization in 1988 to provide world policy makers with scientific assessments regarding climate change, issued a report in 2018 arguing that global temperatures must not rise more than 1.5 degrees Centigrade in order to avoid long-lasting and irreversible changes including the destruction of some ecosystems.[71] They adopted this position even though most policy makers had set themselves a goal of 2 degrees Centigrade (3.5 Fahrenheit) beyond pre-18th century levels.[72]

Indeed, climate scientists warn that even if we do limit global warming to 2 degrees Centigrade, we will already have reached the threshold of a crisis so severe that it threatens our global civilization. The reality we must face is that we have already unleashed forces of climate change that will have severe repercussions for many years to come.

Despite the warnings and the evidence we are already seeing that global warming is a danger that affects all of us, it is also within our control to mitigate, and it provides us with the greatest opportunity we have ever had to learn how to work together toward a vital common goal—planetary survival. Yet, despite multiple attempts to come together as a community of nations and agree on effective ways to stem the unprecedented rise in global temperatures that threatens to decimate our way of life as we know it, our leaders have hitherto been unsuccessful. The latest global attempt to come to some sort of agreement occurred in December 2015 when 195 nations and the European Union came together in Paris for the 21st Conference of the Parties of the United Nations Framework Convention on Climate Change. Their aim was to consult and arrive at a global agreement to reduce greenhouse gas emissions and slow down global warming enough to save our planet from immediate disaster. The meeting was viewed as a make-or-break opportunity. After six years of negotiations, 195 parties signed the Paris Agreement on December 12, 2015, which entered into force on November 4, 2016. Participants at the negotiations finally accepted scientists' warnings that allowing global average temperatures to rise more than 2 degrees Centigrade above pre-industrial levels would be far too dangerous, and they agreed to keep temperatures well below that level. Beyond that, signatories agreed to endeavor to limit temperature increases to 1.5 degrees Centigrade.

While the Paris Agreement represents significant progress, in the estimation of many scientists, it falls significantly short of its ultimate goal of avoiding some of the more catastrophic consequences of climate change. Robert Watson, former chair of the IPCC warned, "The current pledges, even if fully implemented, are placing us on a pathway to a world 3 to 4 degrees Celsius warmer—a world that would have devastating impacts on food and water security, human health, displacement of people, and loss of biodiversity and degradation of ecosystem services, among other impacts."[73] In November 2019, the Alliance of World Scientists, representing 11,000 scientists, published a report warning that the planet was facing a climate emergency.[74] What the world needs are initiatives like a massive, unified effort to tackle climate change by providing both the incentives and funding to research carbon capture quickly and put it in place in time, in order to prevent the world from reaching the tipping point into complete crisis.

Despite the wonderful intentions behind these agreements, our long-standing and maladaptive habit of nationalism raised its ugly head and undermined them. The most glaringly destructive impact of nationalism manifested itself in the unwillingness of participating nations to be bound by clear rules limiting the amount of fossil fuels each nation could burn and the amount of carbon dioxide it could emit. Instead the participants chose to rely on a system of pledges made by individual countries to reduce their greenhouse gas emissions. Unfortunately, this approach has two significant problems. The first is that even if all the pledges were carried out, it is still too little too late because, as a practical matter, it will still result in a roughly 3.5 degree Centigrade increase in global temperatures.

The second problem lies in the poor design of a global system purportedly designed to safeguard the very well-being and security of the planet. Attempting to address what is currently the gravest global challenge facing humanity by relying on a voluntary system of pledges rather than a system of binding and enforceable laws that would require each nation to play its part—all because of our insistence on clinging to our outworn habit of nationalism—is both foolish and shameful. Under the Paris Agreement these pledges are purely voluntary, "nationally determined contributions" (NDCs). There is nothing to stop a country from withdrawing its pledge. Indeed, the temptation is great to sacrifice the pledges to political expediency. Individual politicians will think nothing of reneging on their voluntary promises if they believe that doing so will play to their political base. As different administrations come and go, there is nothing to stop a wild swing in the pendulum between adhering to the voluntary pledges and abandoning them. Indeed, after entering into the Paris Climate Agreement under one administration, the United States has already withdrawn from it under a subsequent administration, demonstrating that it is effectively a contract between states to which members voluntarily accede or from which they can easily withdraw. If the most powerful nation on earth is to do this, what is to stop other countries from following suit?

Moreover, the Paris Agreement does not set specific emission targets for member countries to reach. Rather, it depends on each country to develop plans as to how it will contribute to climate change mitigation on whatever timetable it sees fit, and then to communicate the plans to the secretariat of the convention. Every five years, participating countries are supposed to lodge new NDCs. Although a technical expert group will review information provided by the countries to determine whether they are on track to meet both their individual commitment and the overall objectives of the Paris Agreement, at the end of the day, the NDCs are not binding or enforceable. Indeed, the agreement specifically provides that these reviews are merely "facilitative," "non-intrusive, non-punitive [in] manner," and "respectful of national sovereignty."[75] In other words, these plans are merely promises made by individual countries that may or may not choose to follow through. The third problem lies in the fact that, rather than imposing binding penalties, the agreement relies on regular cycles of reporting and pledging new targets—in other words, the moral persuasion of naming and shaming countries that miss their own voluntary targets. We need to set aside narrowly conceived nationalist interests and try much harder to preserve our climate and save our environment.

U.S.–China Tariff Wars

The results of the dysfunctional habit of nationalism are always destructive—not only for other nations, but also for the nation exhibiting nationalism. A simple example is the effect that the 2018-2020 U.S.–China tariff wars have had on the U.S. economy.[76] The United States has long been frustrated by certain behaviors on the part of China that it considers amount to unfair trade practices. These behaviors include alleged theft of intellectual property, forced transfer of technology to China, and a growing trade deficit. In an effort to change these behaviors and to stimulate manufacturing at home, the United States began to impose a series of tariffs on Chinese exports in 2018. Experts suggest that although the United States boasted that the trade war it initiated would decimate China, what actually happened was that the U.S. economy got hit two and half times worse than China did, causing American manufacturers and consumers to pay tens of billions of dollars more for imported products and parts.[77] While the trade wars took a toll on Chinese manufacturers, U.S. soybean and other farmers suffered the brunt of the damage because China halted all imports of soybeans from the United States.[78] The number of farms that went into bankruptcy rose, as did the amount of debt that farmers took on.

The economic damage wrought by the U.S.–China trade wars was not limited to the two nations who recklessly chose to engage in it. Because of the reality that the economies of all nations are inextricably woven together, some experts were predicting that its prolongation was likely to trigger a global recession. The former head of the International Monetary Fund, Christine Lagarde, asserted her belief that these trade wars and Brexit would be the two biggest risks that would trigger a global recession. It is little surprise that both of these risk factors are born of the habit of nationalism. Little did we know then that a global pandemic would intervene to hasten the advent of such a global recession.

Bridging the Gap Between Where We Are and Where We Want to Be

Our examination of the ways in which our habit of making decisions based on narrowly-conceived national interests—regardless of consequences to other nations—has wrought havoc in our world and contributed to the global lack of peace and security that we face should have demonstrated that the time has come to abandon our old attachment to nationalism.

TAKING STOCK OF WHERE WE ARE

It's time to take stock of where we are. Our reality is that the mindset that globalization is the root problem has gotten us to disunity and fragmentation. We are very far from the vision we want for ourselves—a world that is peaceful, and in which we all are able to develop our potential and thrive. In order to progress and get to that goal, the first step is assessing where we are now with truth and honesty. We can then see what the gap is between where we are and where we want to be and take the steps to bridge that gap.

The reality is that, with this negative mindset about globalization, the cost is too high. Not only is it not getting us to the future that we want, but it is putting us in a position in a time in our collective history when we are faced with several existential crises, like climate change, the pandemic, and the threat of nuclear war, where we are ill-equipped and incapable to act collectively to face these challenges. We both lack the necessary habits of collaboration and cooperation and the institutions for collective decision-making and implementation of our decisions. Our current situation is incredibly dangerous. We must get out of it fast.

REFRAMING OUR MINDSET: THE ONENESS MODEL

So, what will it take to bridge the gap between where we are and where we want to be? This process starts with changing our mindset. Instead of believing that globalization is to blame, we must accept and embrace our interconnectedness. Indeed, not only are we interconnected, but we are interconnected and interdependent to such a degree that the whole world has become one single entity. If we were to take this concept as our new mindset, then we would have a solid foundation upon which to move forward and achieve our goal.

When we don this lens we perceive that—thanks to tremendous advances in communication, transportation, and trade—we have, indeed, become interconnected and interdependent in a manner that is unprecedented. Indeed, our actions are so intertwined that human society can be viewed as a single organism. The community of nations has become like a single body, with each nation representing a different limb or organ. This body is now suffering from severe illness. Just as it would be nonsensical for the heart to say of the kidneys, "I do not care that you are diseased and ailing. I am only concerned with my own well-being," so too, it is futile for any one nation to say that it can function alone without the support and assistance of other nations. The only way to ensure the health of any organ or limb—i.e. any one nation—is by ensuring the health of the entire body.

Once we truly adjust our mindset to understand that all people and nations are limbs and members of a single global body, and that the world is a single organism in which the well-being of the part can only be assured by guaranteeing the well-being and health of the whole, then we arrive at the inevitable conclusion that we must love and care for all the cells and parts of this body equally. Just as there is no point in having healthy organs if we allow our feet to develop gangrene that will affect the entire body and threaten its life, there is no point in taking care of our own kind—whether they are members of our race, ethnicity, or nation—while discriminating against those who seem foreign or different to us.

Ultimately, recognizing our oneness will manifest itself in the degree to which the nations of the world become integrated and unified. Once we adopt the mindset proposed in the previous section that humanity has been on a historical arc of development that is characterized by increasing circles of integration, as demonstrated by the widening circles of loyalty starting with the family, clan, city-state, and nation, we will see that the next inevitable step in our collective growth requires us to achieve unity at a global level. This means that we come to owe our primary loyalty to humanity as a whole rather than to any one group or nation. While these other loyalties are important and have their rightful place, in a world that is as interconnected as ours, they must be subsumed under the demands of a greater loyalty to humanity.

Yet even as we develop our capacity for love and unity of all the parts that make up our world, we also recognize that each part has its own unique and valuable contribution to the whole. Returning to the analogy of humanity as a single body, we recognize that while the lungs and kidneys are different parts of the same body, they each play an important role. Not only do we appreciate those roles, but we also seek to ensure that all the parts of the body are functioning well. Only when the various systems and limbs work efficiently and in coordination with one another is the body able to perform at its peak capacity. The same holds true for differences of thought, culture, appearance, and expression. The diversity of these elements increases both the beauty and the resilience of our communities and nations. Just as walking through a garden in which all the flowers are the same shape, color, height, and fragrance is not nearly as interesting or enjoyable as walking in a garden filled with a variety of different flowers, so too, our communities would lack the vibrancy, creativity, and strength that comes from diversity. Moreover, studies show that the more we expose ourselves to diverse outlooks and ideas, the better we understand our world, and that the very clash that initially can occur when these different cultures and outlooks meet produces the spark that lights the way to approaches and solutions that benefit all those involved.[79] In sum, once we realize that diversity is a symbol of the perfection of humanity we will cease to shun it, and rather than grudgingly tolerate it, we will actively seek it out.

The Importance of Collective Action, Collaboration, and Cooperation

Over the years, circumstances have afforded us ample opportunity to learn the importance of collective action. We have confronted a number of growing global crises that endanger our peace and security. Climate change, migration, the growing extremes of wealth and poverty, and nuclear proliferation rank high among them. And yet, despite the severity of these crises, we have been unwilling to give up our old maladaptive habits of focusing on our self-interest, both on the individual and national levels. We have stubbornly refused to admit that the advantage of the part can only be ensured by guaranteeing the advantage of the whole, and that we are all better off when our primary loyalty is to the entire human race. We have failed to understand that in order to thrive as individuals and nations we must ensure that all nations and all peoples can thrive.

Now, however, the rapid spread of COVID-19 is giving us a unique and unprecedented opportunity to learn this lesson quickly. Indeed, we are being given a crash course in the truth of the oneness of humanity, its inextricable interdependence, and the need for collective action. The stakes are high—it's do or die for many. We can learn—and we are learning—this lesson, albeit slowly. Whether at the city, state, national, or international levels, we are being painfully forced to learn and adapt, kicking and screaming as we go.

While nations have instinctively sought to tackle the spread of the virus and its economic impact by focusing on the well-being of their own citizens—closing borders, ensuring that they have necessary supplies, and blaming other nations for their misfortunes—it is becoming increasingly clear that our only hope for mitigating the suffering of humanity everywhere is by communicating, collaborating, and cooperating together. What if, instead of viewing these same events—including the spreading coronavirus—as looming disasters, we viewed them as an opportunity for humanity to finally learn how to communicate in a spirit of goodwill and transparency, and to cooperate and collaborate on finding workable solutions that benefit us all? What if, instead of viewing other nations and their actions as enemies and threats, we viewed them as indispensable allies with whom to join forces in the fight against a global threat? As *The Washington Post* foreign affairs columnist David Ignatius acknowledged in the early days of COVID-19's spread in the United States, "We sometimes say that a global crisis—a catastrophic natural disaster, say—could unite the planet and encourage everyone to pull together. With coronavirus, we'll have a test of that proposition."[80] The editors of *Nature Medicine* also highlighted the importance of global cooperation, noting that, "Public-health security transcends borders," and that, "In the face of global infectious-disease emergencies, countries have a responsibility to be transparent in their reporting and actions, both to their own populations and to the international community, in order to facilitate and accelerate cooperation that will ultimately curtail outbreaks and minimize harm."[81]

We are slowly coming to the realization that we are only as safe from the virus and as healthy as our weakest link. To the extent that the virus is spreading in any one part of the globe, given the levels of international travel and trade, people everywhere are at risk.

We are beginning to see the first glimmerings of what cooperation and collaboration on an international scale can look like, and the tremendous benefits they can yield in the example that is being set by researchers, doctors, and scientists who are trying to understand the coronavirus and create a vaccine to protect against it. As we have seen, the COVID-19 pandemic has already transformed the way in which scientists communicate and share data about this rapidly spreading disease. The example that these scientists are setting is one that our political leaders would do well to emulate.

Dr. Francesco Perrone, who led a coronavirus clinical trial in Italy, aptly described the mindset of a true scientist by saying, "I never hear scientists—true scientists, good quality scientists—speak in terms of nationality ... My nation, your nation. My language, your language. My geographic location, your geographic location. This is something that is really distant from true top-level scientists."[82] This is the standard that all of us should aspire to, and at the minimum demand of our leaders.

Beyond understanding that we are one because of our interconnectedness, a cardinal lesson we are learning is that humanity is in essence one, regardless of national boundaries. Contrary to the way we behave, the reality is that we share a common identity as human beings. Regardless of our racial, ethnic, or national origins; regardless of our gender, educational attainments, or differences in wealth—we are all human. We all share the same fears and aspirations for ourselves, our families, and our communities. We all wish to have fair and equal access to resources, opportunities, and communities that enable us to thrive and lead lives of meaning and service to others. Most importantly, we are all spiritual beings having a physical experience, and fellow-travelers in a common journey with the common purpose of achieving individual and collective growth. At the individual level we seek to understand and attain our purpose in life and to fulfill our inherent potential. At the societal level we are working toward the creation of a system of governance that creates the necessary conditions for all of us to fulfill our individual and collective potential.

Recognizing That There Are Laws That Govern Our Social Reality

We are slowly and painfully learning the truth that, just as there are laws that govern our physical existence—such as the law of gravity—so too, are there social and spiritual laws that govern our social reality. Although we can choose to ignore these laws, we do so at our peril. Just as we would be foolish to attempt to build an airplane without taking into account the laws of gravity, it would be foolish to expect our social, economic, political, and religious institutions to flourish without taking into account the law of our oneness. We are already witnessing the disastrous consequences of ignoring this law of human life. We are seeing first-hand the collapse of our meticulously-crafted social and institutional infrastructures, most of which ignore humanity's essential oneness. Unless we rapidly adjust our laws, policies, and institutions to take into account this principle of oneness, we will continue to watch them fail and collapse, resulting in tremendous additional suffering. We can, however, stem this tide and reverse it.

The other principle that we must take into account is the law of love. Love is "the vital bond inherent ... in the realities of things"[83] It manifests itself at all levels of creation in the form of unity and integration, while honoring diversity. The vegetable, animal, and human kingdoms all rely on the power of cohesion to survive. If we want to transform our world into one that is peaceful and united, we must create a social reality in which the dominant frequency is love. The more we understand that, in an interconnected world, the interests of all nations are fused into one common interest, the faster we will recognize that the key to solving all of our problems—regardless of what they are—is to integrate our institutional infrastructure to assure the well-being of this single organism. In doing so, we will not seek to erase our diversity. Rather, we will view it as a sign of our perfection and we will move beyond merely tolerating our differences to celebrating them. As we do so, we will begin to benefit from the various strengths that each of us brings to the common interest of humanity as a whole.

Whether we like it or not, interconnectedness is our current reality. Instead of wasting energy fighting this reality, it is time for us to fully accept and embrace it. Only then will we be able to truly see the options before us and to take constructive actions that are conducive to our well-being. While our interconnectedness allows us to derive enormous benefits from rapid global communication, transportation, and trade, we are also more susceptible to systemic risks, such as climate change, pandemics, and global financial crises. This point has been made very eloquently by some theorists including University of Oxford professor Ian Goldin, who observes that while advances in economics, politics, and technology have "led to a step-change in global connectivity," and while "interdependence and innovation have brought unprecedented benefits," including "the most rapid global rise in incomes and health in history," yet, "the same processes of integration and innovation have also greatly increased the potential for systemic risk and global crises."[84]

Reactions to Avoid

Surely, the answer to managing these systemic risks like climate change does not lie in attempting to de-globalize the world. Jeffrey Sachs, world-renowned economist and professor at Columbia University addresses this impulse by saying that globalization, which he defines as "a fact of humanity, a fact of interdependence over large distances," was a process that started 70,000 years ago when modern humans first migrated from Africa. They traded with each other, communicated with each other, fought with each other, migrated, and passed pathogens—all patterns that we see today. He emphasizes that humanity has always been, and will always remain interconnected. Like Goldin, Sachs emphasizes that globalization has brought humanity much good, including the benefits of knowledge and diversity, and he reminds us that while there may be times that globalization is reversed, such reversal is undesirable. Indeed, the times in history when we have tried to stop it and resist it are known as the "Dark Ages." He gives as an example the period after the industrial age in which the Luddites took to smashing agricultural machinery in the early 19th century in England rather than creating social systems that would embrace machines and use them to their benefit. He also points to the Middle—or "Dark"—Ages after the collapse of the Roman Empire when there was a reversal and return to village mentality, resulting in a contraction in European trade and communication.

More recent attempts to de-globalize have generally led to chaos or a rise in militarism. An example of this phenomenon occurred after World War I, when international trade and finance fell into disarray, and from 1931 onward when there was an almost complete collapse in international trade that took a lot of effort to reconstruct after WWll. Sachs also acknowledges that globalization has a dark side and brings with it destructive effects like the rapid spread of pathogens and the unequal distribution of wealth. The answer to this risk, he says, is not to deny the reality of our interconnectedness, but rather to always "be on our guard" to ensure that we address these effects by being prepared for the global crises like climate change and pandemics, and to be "smarter in what we do" to ensure that we find ways to redistribute income more equitably.[85]

The answer, then, does not lie in attempting to undo globalization and hark back to the days of unfettered nationalism and insularity, which maps to what Shawn Achor pointed out was one of our tendencies—namely, to undo progress we have made. Rather, the answer is to ensure that we create the collective decision-making and enforcement institutions that allow us to effectively tackle the global challenges created by our exposure to new systemic risks. Looking at it another way, the egg of human connection has been scrambled and cannot now be unscrambled. Not only is it too late to reverse the trend of globalization, but more importantly, we must ask ourselves why we would want to undo all this progress.

Instead, what we can and must do as soon as possible is catch up to our reality by building the infrastructure of global governance necessary to tackle the systemic risks and global challenges of our time, starting with the most severe and existential ones such as the COVID-19 pandemic, climate change, and the threat of nuclear war.[86]

The days of acting unilaterally and obstructing collective action have long passed. It is becoming increasingly evident that these are self-defeating strategies. For instance, individualism has long been a central obstacle to successfully tackling climate change. One striking example of the harmfulness of individualism occurred at the March 2019 U.N. Environment Assembly meeting held in Nairobi. According to reporting by *The Economist* magazine at the time, the Swiss had put on the agenda a couple of proposals for conducting an international assessment of the positive and negative effects of using geoengineering and various technologies to reverse global warming.[87] The ideas included using a planetary sunshade that would reduce global temperatures, akin to the effects produced by the ash spewed into the atmosphere after the 1991 volcanic eruption of Mount Pinatubo in the Philippines that cooled the world's atmosphere by up to 0.5 degrees Centigrade for four years. Another idea was to use technology to pull carbon dioxide out of the atmosphere and store it. Both proposals required collective agreement and action in order to be viable. However, the United States and Saudi Arabia opposed the idea of even having the international community conduct an investigation and produce a report about the feasibility of using geoengineering methods. Some delegates reported that the Americans "did not appear to want to make room for conversations, let alone make decisions, about a framework for geoengineering that could restrict their future options," despite the universality of the restrictions. Both countries vetoed the inclusion of the proposals on the agenda. Consequently, the proposals were removed and not presented to the 170 participating nations for consideration.

What this example—among many others—highlights is that the world needs to recognize that while many of our problems are global and collective in nature, therefore requiring collective action and solutions, we lack the very collective decision-making and enforcement institutions we so desperately need to tackle these challenges. While human society has evolved by leaps and bounds in many arenas, such as science and technology, our institutions of global governance are seriously lagging behind and we are now suffering from what has come to be known as a global governance gap. It is time we filled this gap by building global institutions fit for the 21st century and beyond. We must also identify a set of global ethics to be woven into the very fabric of these institutions and to be used by them as a starting point when attempting to solve global challenges.

CHOOSING A NEW HABIT: BUILDING A SYSTEM OF GLOBAL GOVERNANCE

The starting point for identifying the new constructive habit that can replace nationalism is to adjust our collective perspective and mindset about our social reality. As we have stated before, it has become abundantly clear that our world is interconnected in unprecedented ways. This interconnectedness is not going to change, and no matter how much some people may wish they could reverse this reality, there is no going back.

One of the best ways of envisioning our interdependence is to consider a brilliant analogy offered by Professor

Kishore Mahbubani, a long-time Singaporean diplomat and dean of the Lee Kuan Yew School of Public Policy in Singapore. He observed that, not long ago, the nations of the world were like self-contained boats sailing on the sea of international life. Each boat had its own captain and crew, and the main purpose of the international order was to create rules that ensured that the movements of these boats were coordinated to avoid accidents. However, over time that reality shifted. Our current reality is completely different. Given the unprecedented degree of our interconnectedness, our situation could more aptly be described as that of a ship consisting of 193 cabins, each representing a nation state. However, while each cabin has its own captain and crew dedicated to maintaining order and serving the people within it, the ship as a whole lacks both captain and crew.

In a time of global crisis, such as the world faces with the COVID-19 pandemic, there is no one at the helm of our ship capable of steering us in stormy and turbulent seas. Nor do we have hands on deck dedicated to the collective good—the business of saving the ship as a whole —rather than the narrow well-being of the members of one of the cabins onboard. Furthermore, the principles and rules by which the inhabitants in one cabin govern themselves could actually prove detrimental to people in other cabins and could cause the ship as a whole to sink. It is not hard to recognize how this plays out in the context of the COVID-19 pandemic, where actions taken by one national government—such as restricting the export of medical supplies or cornering the market on a successful vaccine—detrimentally impact the citizens of other nations.

For humanity to survive and thrive all of this must change. As we have seen, our most intractable challenges are collective in nature. Consequently, they demand collective solutions. Over the years, circumstances have afforded us ample opportunity to learn the importance of collective action. We have confronted a number of growing global crises that endanger our peace and security. Climate change, migration, the threat of pandemics, the growing extremes of wealth and poverty, and nuclear proliferation rank high among them. And yet, despite the severity of these crises, we have been unwilling to give up our old maladaptive habits of focusing on our self-interest, both on the individual and national levels. We have stubbornly refused to admit that the advantage of the part can only be ensured by guaranteeing the advantage of the whole, and that we are all better off when our primary loyalty is to humanity as a whole. We have failed to understand that if we are to thrive as individuals and nations we must ensure that all nations and all peoples can thrive.

Consequently, despite the fact that collective challenges demand collective solutions, we find ourselves lacking the very collective decision-making and enforcement institutions the world needs to effectively and efficiently address these global challenges.

We need to swiftly craft global decision-making institutions. Furthermore, these institutions must have the authority to pass binding regulations to protect us in certain narrow spheres where the only solution lies in collective action. We also need global enforcement mechanisms to ensure that all nations comply with these collective rules. In order to create this new system of global governance, we must first acknowledge that the heyday of nationalism is long past. Today's global reality demands that all nations be willing to subordinate their nationalistic impulses to the requirements of a unified and inextricably interconnected world.

While some voices have for many years been calling for the creation of a limited form of global government, most of our leaders have been unwilling to countenance such an idea. Yet, finally, in the face of the enormous physical, economic, and mental suffering we have begun enduring in the COVID-19 pandemic, we are starting to hear voices among the world's leaders calling for the creation of some kind of system of global governance that is capable of responding to the needs of the 21st century. Such voices should be encouraged and applauded.

Spanish Minister of Foreign Affairs, European Union and Cooperation, Arancha González Laya, expressed her view in a piece published by *The Washington Post* in March 2020, that it is "time to be bold and envision new ways forward for our international institutions."[88] She clearly articulated the goal: "to find ways to reinforce the institutions that work, replace those that do not, create those that are missing and, overall, promote simplicity, effectiveness, coherence and cohesion."

A day later, Gordon Brown, the former prime minister of Britain clearly outlined the need for an international response to the coronavirus crisis in an article published by *The Guardian*.[89] He cut straight to the chase, urging world leaders "to create a temporary form of global government to tackle the twin medical and economic crises caused by the Covid-19 pandemic." He also highlighted the obvious yet often unacknowledged fact that, "this is not something that can be dealt with in one country," rather, it is something that requires "a coordinated global response," starting with "some sort of working executive."

What an incredible call to action! This is precisely the kind of leadership we need—one that is willing to acknowledge and dispense with systems that are not working and that no longer ensure the well-being of the people they were created to serve, and one that recognizes the need for collective consultation in order to conceive of new global structures capable of managing collective problems that impact humanity as a whole.

This kind of call confirms world historian Arnold Toynbee's predictions in the last century that, despite our strenuous resistance to any notion of a world government, once we faced an existential threat we would rapidly, though reluctantly, abandon our resistance in favor of a world government, and move toward the creation of such a government. Interestingly, he thought that the existential threat that would bring us to this point would be the atomic bomb. While the atomic bomb has not generated a shift toward reimagining global governance, perhaps recent threats such as COVID-19 will provide the necessary impetus.

The COVID-19 pandemic is affording us a golden opportunity to come to our senses and create the kind of global government we so desperately need to assure our peace, well-being, and security. However, we still have the power of volition. If we allow ourselves to become complacent we could forfeit this incredible opportunity to use the coronavirus as a stepping-stone toward a better world and a better future. If that were to happen, we would undoubtedly continue to be buffeted by the storms of ever-growing and intensifying global challenges until we come to our senses and create a unified system of global governance fit to address the needs of the 21st century and beyond.

We have a choice to mitigate our global suffering and to ensure that our hardships have not been in vain. It is up to us, one and all, to demand of our leaders that they seize this opportunity to demonstrate the statesmanship, vision, and courage required to build the global decision-making and enforcement institutions that we so desperately need to meet the urgent needs of an inextricably interconnected world. We can no longer satisfy ourselves with the institutions and social structures that we have. We must, instead, be willing and courageous enough to envision what we want and what could be, and then work with ceaseless effort to make that vision a reality.

World Parliament

Once we accept that we ought to start building an infrastructure composed of global decision-making institutions, where do we begin? If we are serious about being able to solve our global problems, then we must be willing to create a world parliament that is truly representative of the peoples of the world and that has the authority to pass binding legislation on all nations in certain specific arenas that affect all of humanity and that cannot be solved by any one nation alone.

The members of this parliament should be directly elected by the people of each country in proportion to that country's population, and confirmed by their respective governments. Doing so will ensure that people everywhere have a voice in the collective decision-making process that ensures the well-being of humanity. In other words, the parliament will have democratic legitimacy. Knowing that their voices are heard will, in turn, inspire people everywhere with confidence and trust in the decisions and laws made by the parliament, and people will be more willing to abide by them.

The parliament will have the authority to enact such global legislation in areas of human activity that affect the collective interests of all nations and are necessary to regulate the relationships of all peoples and nations and address their common challenges and needs. Other decisions that concern individual nations will continue to be decided at the national level. In light of COVID-19 one can imagine that such laws might include some regulations to ensure that the world is prepared for future outbreaks of a pandemic. These regulations might include provision for a robust early warning system, requirements that each nation have certain stockpiles of personal protective equipment, and a plan for activating manufacturing capabilities to ensure that the material that is needed to face a given pandemic can be produced quickly and equitably distributed. The regulations should also lay out processes for allocating funding, for ensuring collaborative research, and for joint production of and equitable access to vaccines and viable treatments. Moreover, the parliament should be able to pass regulations harmonizing the response systems of various nations in a time of crisis, understanding that in a time of global crisis, the needs of all nations must be equitably met because we are only as strong as our weakest link. The parliament must play the role of captain of the ship of the global community in times of crisis, guiding the ship of humanity to safe harbor.

Another potential area in which the world parliament can act is passing a modicum of financial regulation to protect us from the types of financial crises to which we have become prone. This regulation would again take into account the needs of all nations on a just and equitable basis and ensure that in times of global economic crisis individual nations do not respond with patchwork decisions that may at first blush appear to serve their national interests, but that effectively operate to the detriment of other nations, and over the long-term to the detriment of the entire global community.

The sphere of laws that such a parliament could pass might also include regulation of the types and amounts of energy each country can use to ensure that we do not continue to pollute our environment and create problems like global warming that threaten us with disaster. They could also include food and water regulation to ensure that everyone has fair access to sufficient clean water and nutrition. Such laws would also contain rules on arms production and proliferation, including the ability to pass legislation banning the manufacture of all weapons of mass destruction and requiring the destruction of all such existing weapons.

In addition to its powers to pass global legislation, this legislature will also take on certain rights that have historically been vested in states. States must willingly cede these jurisdictions because they understand that doing so best serves their national and collective global interest. Such rights include all rights to make war and to use force as an instrument of international relations. They also include all rights to maintain arms except in the amount necessary to maintain internal order within national borders. The world parliament would have the authority to determine, after careful study, perhaps by a commission it appoints, the proper amount of arms each nation requires in order to maintain internal peace and order. All arms in excess of that determined amount should be destroyed under the watchful supervision of the parliament as a means of ensuring transparency and confidence in the system on the part of all nations. The motivating factor driving this requirement is that any increase in military forces by one nation will only serve to arouse the suspicion of other states, who will then take steps they deem necessary to retaliate and redress the balance. So begins the well-known problem of an arms race, with all the attendant rises in tension and the possibility of unintended accidents. Our world is all too familiar with this scenario—the Cold War was largely a study in precisely this phenomenon, leading us to the ludicrous comfort point of mutually assured destruction. Nations will also cede to the parliament all rights to make war. This means that the nations will forego the use of force as an instrument of international relations and as a means of resolving their disputes. Meanwhile the world legislature must use force only collectively and in service of justice.

The nations will also cede to the parliament limited authority to impose taxes, affording that institution the funds to uplift and better the condition of humanity. Just as many of us pay taxes at the local and national levels, we would also all be required to pay taxes for this international fund. It is easy to imagine that such funds would be used to find ways of reversing or ameliorating global warming or to find alternative sources of clean and renewable energy. The funds could also be used to relocate refugees displaced by rising oceans, thereby relieving some of the intense economic strains currently imposed on those refugees and on the countries that receive them. The funds would also be used to provide bail-out funds or financial assistance to countries that find themselves in dire economic straits. The beauty of this system of funding bail-outs is that when their use becomes necessary, wealthier nations will not feel like they are always called upon to unfairly support their poorer neighbors. Rather, all peoples and nations will have contributed their fair share to the bail-out funds and feel like that they have a stake in the system. Consequently, they will have a vested interest in making sure that they behave in financially responsible ways. These funds can also be used to support relief efforts in response to natural disasters like pandemics, earthquakes, floods, cyclones, hurricanes, starvation, drought, or floods as well as funding the creation and maintenance of an international standing force to preserve peace in the world.

One of the critical powers of the world parliament arises from the fact that nations must grant it complete and exclusive authority over the earth's resources in its capacity as the trustee of the whole of humanity, including many resources that may as yet be undiscovered and untapped. The parliament will then have the exclusive responsibility for developing, managing, and distributing all critical natural resources for the benefit of humanity as a whole. These resources could well include energy, water, and food. To this end, it will have the sole authority to tap and fully utilize these resources. It will also organize all the economic resources of the world, coordinating and developing the global markets and ensuring that the distribution of products is equitably regulated based on legitimate need. In short, the world parliament will exercise unchallengeable authority over the vast resources of the whole earth, and it will bend its energies to the use of all the available resources for the benefit of all. By granting the world parliament such authority we would prevent and eradicate a large number of conflicts in which we currently engage in our quest for such resources such as oil, gas, clean water, and food.

In this context, it is important to note that, in order to discharge its mandate effectively, the world parliament must have at its disposal vast sums of money that have hitherto been wasted on weapons, war, and all other military expenditures. According to the Stockholm International Peace Research Institute, that amount grew to $1.97 trillion in 2019.[90]

Indeed, the parliament would only need a fraction of that amount to meet the basic needs of humanity. Moreover, it will also be able to harness the enormous political energy historically wasted on conflict and war.

Effective World Court

Once nations have ceded all rights to make war to the world parliament, it becomes even more crucial for them to have an effective mechanism to resolve their disputes. Even in the most closely-knit families, family members will inevitably disagree, sometimes intensely. Healthy, mature families find ways of managing and resolving their disputes amicably. Dysfunctional families allow disputes to engender long-term resentment, bitterness, anger, and even outright violent conflict. If we accept the analogy that humanity grows and matures like an individual, it stands to reason that at this stage in humanity's maturation process the world's nations can also find increasingly mature ways to resolve their inevitable disagreements and disputes peaceably, without resorting to force.

An effective world court can serve as such an institution whose role is to contribute to the establishment and maintenance of universal peace by acting as the first port of call for conflict resolution between nations and other constituent elements of the international system that have found other means of resolution ineffective. By referring conflicts to a world court for final resolution, nations will no longer resort to using force to resolve their disputes.

Fortunately, experience has already taught us a number of crucial lessons about what it will take to create a successful world court. In the aftermath of World War I, the community of nations created an International Tribunal as an agency of the League of Nations, in the hopes that nations would turn to it to resolve their disputes instead of shedding unnecessary blood in destructive wars. They hoped that the tribunal would thereby maintain peace in the world. When both the tribunal and the League of Nations failed, and the world suffered the horrors of a second World War, the community of nations picked itself up and tried again, creating the United Nations and an International Court of Justice (ICJ) to support it. Unfortunately, however, the ICJ's creation contained certain fatal flaws in its structure that hamper its ability to maintain peace.

These flaws have taught us that for a world court to be effective, several conditions must prevail. First, the manner in which the court's judges are elected must inspire trust. The judges must be truly representative of the peoples of the world, fully competent, free of bias, and independent of the wishes of any particular nation or group of nations. They must be fair-minded and interested in rendering just and equitable decisions untainted by political pressure. At the moment, the judges of the ICJ secure appointments from their countries in back room deals heavily influenced by political considerations, rather than having the collective interests of humanity as the driving motive in their selection. Indeed, studies have shown that existing ICJ judges often exercise bias in favor of their own countries when deciding cases. As a result, the decisions of the ICJ do not always represent humanity's unalloyed interests of peace and justice. The following recommended changes should create the conditions for a new world court that inspires trust.

All parliaments of the world should be required to elect two or three representatives who are highly regarded and distinguished in their country. The precise number of those elected should be proportionate to the population of that country. They should be well versed in international law and international relations and aware of the essential needs and requirements of the world. Their election should be confirmed by all the component parts of the legislature, including the upper house of parliament or the congress. It should also be confirmed by the executive branch, including the cabinet, and either the president or monarch. In this manner those elected will truly represent both the people and the government. Members of the world court should then be elected from among the entire body of representatives elected around the world. Details of how this election will be conducted and who will be entitled to vote for the members of the world court can be decided by world leaders.

The second condition that must be met for the court to be effective is that it must have compulsory jurisdiction. At present when a nation breaks international laws or otherwise becomes embroiled in serious disputes with another nation, it has the power to decide whether it wants to submit to the jurisdiction of the ICJ or not. This must change. The revamped world court must have the absolute authority to adjudicate all disputes between nations, even when the parties concerned do not voluntarily agree to submit their case to its jurisdiction. Moreover, all of its judgments must be viewed as final and binding on the component parts of the international system.

The third condition is that all of the decisions of the court must be enforceable. Without a mechanism with which to enforce its decisions the court would be toothless and would lack legitimacy. Its judgments would stand in danger of being rendered meaningless in the face of willful disregard and blatant impunity, or even mere delay and dilatory action on the part of recalcitrant nations. It would then be unable to play its vital role of maintaining peace and security and of resolving disputes so that the parties do not resort to violent means for their solution. Indeed, this is precisely the case at present. As it currently stands, even if a nation agrees to accept the jurisdiction of the ICJ, the court has no way of enforcing its final judgment and must rely on the good will of the aggressor to voluntarily abide by the ICJ's decision. No wonder, then, that the ICJ has failed in its purpose to avoid conflicts and wars and to assure world peace.

We would never stand for such a system in our home countries or localities. Imagine the following: a man commits murder in your community, and gets to choose whether or not he wishes to submit to the jurisdiction of the local court to have his case tried. Imagine further that, having acquiesced to trial by such a court, the accused is found guilty and the judge assumes that he will voluntarily abide by the verdict. The judge then tells him to walk himself over to the prison and ask the guards to incarcerate him. Such scenarios seem ludicrous. And yet, this exactly describes the kind of system we currently have in place to serve the world community of nations.

By contrast, under the new system proposed here, not only would the world court have the authority to decide all cases of disputes between nations that might disturb the peace, but in the event that a nation neglects its duty to implement the court's binding decisions promptly and effectively, all nations should be able to collectively enforce the court's judgment, relying upon the international standing force discussed below.

International Executive and Standing Force

We all understand the phenomenon of the bully on the playground. He engenders fear in the hearts of his potential victims, who never know when they will be his next target. Meanwhile, the bully seems quite happy. His tyranny satisfies his emotional need for power and his other more tangible desires—he can get the pen he covets or his fellow classmate's sweatshirt that he has been eyeing. He seems unbeatable, until one day, his schoolmates on the playground decide that they have had enough and unite to stand up to him. In the face of such decisive and overwhelming unity, the bully has no choice but to back down and retreat. The playground, once again, becomes a safe and inviting place. Bullies act out time and again in the global arena, but only rarely do nations unite to face and stop the aggressor. Often, this lack of action is because of the self-interest of individual nations, as we have previously discussed. The only way to combat this nationalistic mindset and successfully triumph over the bullies on the international scale is through creating an international executive and standing force in our proposed system of global governance.

Our world has more than its fair share of nation states that play the role of the bully in the international arena. They build nuclear arms that threaten peace in flagrant contravention of agreed-upon international laws. They commit human rights atrocities on an unimaginable scale, deliberately decimating segments of their population in wanton acts of genocide and in violation of international norms. They colonize and assert territorial control over lands that do not belong to them because these lands contain natural resources that they covet, or because they want to broaden their sphere of influence. But the community of nations suffers from repeated paralysis in the face of such destructive behavior.

In order to end this destructive cycle, our new system of global governance must include within its scope an international executive that represents all nations and acts in their collective interests to preserve world peace. The executive would have the authority to implement and enforce the international legislation enacted by the world parliament in areas that affect the collective interests of all nations. It would also have the authority to enforce decisions of the world court, thereby ensuring that the world has a way to peacefully resolve disputes between nations. These powers are essential. There is no point in passing international laws for the benefit of all peoples if we have no means of enforcing them. Similarly, regardless of how wise and well-considered the judgments of a world court are, they are useless if we lack the means to put them into action. Moreover, the international executive would generally be tasked to deal with any threats to or breaches of the peace, thereby safe-guarding the organic unity of the world.

To achieve these purposes, we must create an international standing force, composed of armed forces representing all the nations of the world. This international military force will act at the behest of the international executive and in accordance with laws and criteria that all nations agree upon in advance. It will act in the collective interests of humanity to preserve the peace and enforce international laws and the judgments of the world court.

We can easily imagine the benefits of such a system. Experts have concluded that it is cheaper to create and maintain an international standing force than for individual nations and the United Nations to fund military interventions as they seek to maintain peace around the world. Such a system would spread the costs among all nations without imposing a disproportionate burden on any single nation.

The deterrent value of such a system is also very high. A bullying aggressor nation would be far less likely to engage in behavior destructive to the peace of the world if it knows that the community of nations has both the will and the means to stand up to it. Moreover, in the face of such collective will and enforcement mechanisms, a bully nation can no longer succeed in pitting other nations against each other, rendering them impotent in the face of its destructive behavior by accusing them of nefarious motives like religious prejudice or a bid to control energy resources.

Finally, a standing army can act quickly and effectively at the first sign of trouble to maintain the peace without allowing the problem to fester and grow unwieldy.

Imagine how much more peaceful and secure our world could be if we built the kind of global decision-making and enforcing institutions proposed here. Given that the gravest crises facing humanity today are global and collective in nature, it stands to reason that the solutions must also be crafted collectively. Yet, we lack the requisite infrastructure in the form of such collective decision-making institutions. Having tried so many other solutions to no avail, is it not time we gave this solution a chance?

The U.N. As It Stands Does Not Fit the Bill

Many people believe or assume that the United Nations can and will stem the tide of these global challenges and provide the global solutions we so urgently need. This, however, is a mistaken belief. The truth is that the U.N. was created in a different era and was not equipped with the power, authority, legitimacy or tools it needs to properly address severe global challenges on the order of climate change, global financial crises, pandemics, terrorism, migration, genocide, or the proliferation of nuclear weapons. As time passed, unfortunately, it failed to evolve as rapidly and drastically as was necessary to meet these challenges. Consequently, unless it is able and willing to radically transform itself at a rapid clip, it stands in danger of becoming obsolete.

The U.N. in its present form is not up to the task of managing acute common problems and does not function with the aforementioned institutions, powers, and authorities critical to building a new system of global governance fit for the 21st century and beyond.

Firstly, the U.N. General Assembly, though it provides a wonderful forum for representatives of nation states to gather on a regular basis to consult upon and discuss global affairs, suffers from two obvious defects. First, its members are not truly representative of the peoples of the world, in that they are not directly elected by global citizens as members of a national parliament or legislature would be elected by national constituents. The institution therefore does not have the democractic legitimacy it requires when it passes resolutions urging action in a particular sphere of activity. Second, the General Assembly does not have the power to pass legislation that is legally binding on all of its member states. Despite its best intentions, it cannot take direct action because it can only pass resolutions that call on individual nations to do so. The General Assembly relies on the hope that nations will take its recommendations seriously enough to act on them. Otherwise it has no power to pass and enforce legislation. Consequently, at a time in our collective history when we most need a viable, collective decision-making body that can effectively address collective challenges, we find ourselves lacking. Moreover, while there are a number of recent proposals calling for some measure of reform of the General Assembly, including an International Parliamentary Union, an International Parliamentary Network, and a United Nations Parliamentary Assembly, unfortunately none of them go far enough to give the General Assembly the binding authority it needs to address the severe global challenges of today.

Furthermore, the Security Council, which is tasked with maintaining peace and security in the world, suffers from several critical flaws. For one, it is not truly representative of the nations of the world. It is also hamstrung by the fact that its five permanent members have the right to veto a decision in support of restoring or maintaining peace, even if all the other nations believe that it is a good decision. The Security Council's mandate is vague and needs to be properly fleshed out so that it can act swiftly and with confidence, knowing that it will not be accused of overstepping its authority. It also lacks some critical tools it needs to accomplish its mission of maintaining peace in the world. For example, it lacks an international intelligence agency from which it can obtain timely, reliable, and transparent information on the basis of which it can make decisions to take action. It also lacks an international police force serving at its behest to take timely, efficient, and effective action to deal with problems before they fester into unwieldy disasters.

Finally, the U.N. today lacks the ability to forestall many global conflicts because of the weakness of the ICJ. As it stands, the Court lacks compulsory jurisdiction to require nations that are in dispute to come before it so it can hear and decide these cases before they spill over into conflict that destabilize peace. It is untenable that at this moment in history when there is so much at stake, and what seem like internal and contained conflicts can so easily cascade into international conflicts with potentially horrific consequences—including the use of nuclear weapons—nations are not compelled to appear before a world court to have their disputes decided peacefully.

Not only does the ICJ lack compulsory jurisdiction, but it also lacks the ability to enforce its decisions and it essentially relies on the honor system for states to comply with its rulings. As discussed above, despite the fact that our world is now so interconnected and interdependent, we continue to put up with this manifestly ridiculous system that is not serving us well. It is high time that we create an international court with both the power of compulsory jurisdiction to hear cases that could lead to international disputes and the means of enforcing its decisions through the agency of an international police force.

Ultimately, the larger lesson here is that if policies and procedures or global institutions, such as the U.N., are no longer serving the welfare of humanity as a whole, and if our systems of global governance are lagging far behind the movement towards global integration and interdependence, then we must be willing either to radically reform them or to create alternatives that will ensure our peace, security, and well-being. We owe this to ourselves and to future generations.

Additional Conditions

Before we consider our next dysfunctional global habit, a word should be said about two conditions that must be met when establishing this new system of global governance. The first is that we must guard against the evils of excessive centralization. We can do so by ensuring that the principle of subsidiarity is mindfully applied. Subsidiarity requires that each decision be made at the level that is most appropriate: local, regional, national, or global. It is important that a healthy balance is established between the powers and authorities of these institutions of global governance to control the destiny of the peoples of the world and those of their local, regional, and national elected institutions. This is why we have stressed all along that the powers and authority of the global institutions must be limited to certain narrow spheres that affect the collective interests of humanity like climate change and pandemics. In most cases, decisions should be able to be made at the domestic level.

The second condition is to encourage unity in diversity and guard against any tendency to impose unity in uniformity. Both experience and research has shown that the more diverse and inclusive decision-making is, the better the outcomes. This is true both in business and in government. In business the evidence clearly points to the fact that decisions are made faster and lead to better business performance and financial gain. Ensuring that people in decision-making positions reflect a diverse range of values, interests, perspectives, and experiences dilutes the inevitable inherent biases of individuals and creates more fertile ground for innovative solutions. The same holds true for governmental institutions, where drawing on different types of knowledge and a broad array of opinions makes room for assumptions in decision-making processes to be challenged.[91]

If we are to build new institutions of global governance fit to address the complex and global needs of twenty-first century society then it is crucial that we ensure they reflect the diversity of human society. Such diversity should be affirmatively sought and welcomed. It should be regarded as a source of strength and resilience and as an effective mechanism to better understand the relevant factors involved in any decision.

OLD MINDSET 5: THE ENDS JUSTIFY THE MEANS

In today's world, many people and leaders believe and act on the premise that the ends to which they are striving justify the means they employ to achieve these ends. The consequence of this mindset is that people in decision-making positions—whether in business, families, government, religious, or social institutions—impose their decisions on people around them by dint of their forceful personalities, or through bullying, manipulation or threat. They justify their behavior on the grounds that the benefit of the end result excuses any harm done along the way. Even if the end goals are well-intentioned, the results of using unequally worthy means are usually extremely harmful.

One example of harmful means used to achieve a supposedly beneficial goal is governmental use of torture to extract information from prisoners who are deemed as threats to national security. Although protecting national security seems like a positive goal, inflicting pain on others in the name of achieving this aim is not only ineffective, but also unnecessarily inhumane. Studies into the C.I.A.'s use of "enhanced interrogation techniques" have time and again demonstrated that interrogation tactics based on fear and torture fail to elicit truthful statements from subjects, therefore rendering this process useless to the final goal. More importantly, using violence and degrading techniques erodes the social fabric of our society. We are striving to create a world in which the nobility of all people is upheld, and in which collaboration is valued above conflict and harm. Resorting to torture and violence is inconsistent with this vision of humanity as a mature entity. Even if such strategies do contribute to the final goal, their negative long-term impacts are far more harmful and unsustainable.

OLD HABIT OF EXPEDIENCY

When we stop to consider our typical response to a global challenge we notice that our knee-jerk response is to find a solution based on this type of short-termism. If nationalism is one of our most baneful collective habits, then short-termism, or expediency, runs a close second. Indeed, the two often go hand in hand.

What do we mean by expediency? In essence, expedient solutions have two defining features. First, they are reactive—we lurch from crisis to crisis, attempting to put out the fire of the day. Second, they are based on a consideration of short-term benefits without regard to long-term consequences. In addition, as already noted, expediency often presents itself in the company of the habit of nationalism, which results in a solution that is based on a narrowly-conceived national self-interest that fails to take into account the broader common interests of an interconnected humanity.

There are a number of destructive consequences that flow from making collective decisions based on expediency. One of these is that we never get to the root of any of our global problems and successfully solve them. Instead we content ourselves with temporarily extinguishing the flames while the embers continue to smolder, waiting for the gusts of wind occasioned by the next crisis to restart the fire. How many times have we seen this phenomenon play out with repeated genocides, despite our loud promises of "Never again!" Nuclear proliferation and illegal nuclear weapons programs proceed apace despite our protestations that they must stop. The number of forcibly displaced people and refugees worldwide stands at 70 million people as of the time of writing, and is greater than it's ever been, with no end in sight to this heart-wrenching global crisis.[92] Financial crises recur with greater ferocity, and now we are in the thick of a devastating COVID-19 pandemic without adequate preparation.

Another damaging consequence is that our solutions to one problem often sow the seeds of the next disaster. In the misguided belief that we are acting to solve the problem at hand, we often end up spawning myriad new problems that tend to be more severe than the original one. Examples of misguided expediency in international relations abound. For instance, during the 1980s the United States encouraged Islamist fundamentalists gathering in Afghanistan to resist first the occupying military forces of the Soviet Union, then an Afghan government widely viewed as a Soviet puppet. Unfortunately, once the Soviet-installed government dissolved, those same fundamentalists spawned the Taliban movement that ultimately led to military intervention by the United States in 2001 to oust them. The United States consequently mired itself in a conflict that continues to this day, with absolutely devastating consequences for Afghanistan. It is hoped that a peace deal that was signed between the United States and the Taliban in February 2020 will lead to the withdrawal of US troops by late spring of 2021, assuming that the sides follow through on their commitments.[93]

Iraq provides us with another example. For years the world allowed Saddam Hussein's government to get away with murder and human rights violations within its own country. This served the perceived commercial interests of some nations and the strategic interests of others that saw in Iraq a counterbalance to Iran, whose influence they feared. Ultimately, two wars were fought and much blood was shed to address the problems caused by Hussein, including his invasion of neighboring Kuwait.

A third, more insidious consequence of expediency is that our solutions to various global challenges are often incongruent with each other and end up undermining each other. In a quest to lock up much-needed oil resources, a country will agree to overlook the gross human rights abuses perpetrated by another country, as China did during the genocide in Darfur, warning that it would veto any attempt by the Security Council to formally declare the killings in Darfur a genocide.

It is worth looking at a few more recent examples of problem-solving based on short-termism to further illustrate the widespread and disastrous consequences of problem-solving based on this outworn habit.

The first involves the decision by the Ecuadorian government to build a dam to help the country meet its energy needs and help lift its population out of poverty.[94] To achieve this goal, Ecuador borrowed vast sums of money from China. Unfortunately, in their eagerness to do the deal, neither Ecuador nor China paid adequate attention to the fact that the dam was built just below a volcano. Consequently, only two years after the dam was completed there already were 7,000 cracks in its machinery. In addition, large amounts of silt, trees, and bushes were piling up in its reservoir, rendering it ineffective. Not only did the completed dam fail to achieve the goal of alleviating poverty, but the Ecuadorian government soon discovered that it did not have the means to repay its debt to China. In the end, Ecuador ended up worse off than it was before it embarked on this venture. Its energy needs are still unmet and China now gets to keep 80 percent of Ecuador's most valuable export, oil, making Ecuador even poorer than it was to begin with.

The second example involves reports of Russia's intensive activities over the past couple of years to enter into agreements with various African countries under which it provides them with arms and military service contracts in return for receiving lucrative mineral extraction contracts as well as diplomatic support in the form of votes in the U.N. General Assembly.[95] So many damaging consequences flow from this pattern of behavior, including increasing the quantity of arms in a world that is already armed to the teeth, raising even further the risk of armed conflict and war. In addition, as though the credibility of international institutions like the United Nations were not damaged enough and trust in them not already ebbing, the whole idea of buying votes undermines the very purpose of the existence of such institutions rendering them corrupt and incapable of serving any useful purpose.

The third example stems from media reports that China has been engaging in activities that wreak environmental havoc just across its border in Russia while forbidding those very same activities within its own borders. Apparently China learned from bitter experience that allowing uncontrolled logging within its borders led to devastating environmental consequences including deforestation, pollution of its lakes and rivers, damaged watersheds and devastating floods. Consequently, it took aggressive steps to restrict commercial logging of its woodlands so as to arrest environmental degradation. Yet, it still has a high demand for wood and has resorted to satisfying this appetite by engaging in intense commercial logging activities across the border in Russia. Moreover, the Russian government has been complicit in the destruction of its own forests and the pollution of its environment: it has been selling logging rights to Chinese companies at a low cost while also turning a blind eye to illegal logging. What makes the behavior of both these countries so surprising is their incredible shortsightedness, since they already suffer from global warming accelerated by such logging.[96]

Short-termism is one of our long-entrenched, dysfunctional habits. For decades we have ignored the glaring evidence that it is an outworn habit that does not serve our well-being. Interestingly, the COVID-19 pandemic is now teaching us, albeit painfully, that we simply can't do business as usual anymore. It is time to change our collective dysfunctional habits, chief among them the habit of acting expediently to solve global challenges. Prolonging a universal crisis that is playing out across the world is forcing us to think ahead, plan proactively for a time when we can emerge out of a global lockdown, and revive our battered economies. We need to do all this while also preparing for and contending with a second and third wave of infections caused by the coronavirus and while finding and distributing treatments and vaccines. While the pandemic is undoubtedly painful it is also providing us a golden opportunity to change our ways, including dispensing with the habit of short-termism once and for all.

ACCEPTING WHERE WE ARE

Before we can move forward and create a better world in which our peace and well-being are assured we must fully embrace our responsibility for the sorry state in which we now find ourselves. Our knee-jerk, unmindful reliance on the habit of short-termism to address the needs and problems of our age has been disastrous. Not only have we failed to solve existing problems at their root, but our short-sighted attempts to solve them have also spawned a host of new problems. Unfortunately, given the multiplicity and gravity of these problems, many of which have global impacts, and the capacity of any one of these threats to annihilate us, it is evident that we cannot go on as before. We cannot continue to do business as usual. Short-termism is unsustainable. The stakes are too high and the costs we must bear in terms of human suffering and despair too severe. Our only hope now is to adopt a new mindset that will redirect our energies towards a more constructive and empowering habit to replace our outmoded habit of short-termism.

REFRAMING OUR MINDSET: THE CONSISTENCY RULE

The new mindset requires accepting and acknowledging that the means we adopt to attain our collective goals are just as important as, if not more important than attaining the goals themselves. After all, it's the quality of the journey that matters in life rather than arrival at the destination. At the end of the day, life itself is a journey, rather than a meaningless movement toward a destination. We feel and are fulfilled only to the extent that the journey has been conducive to our growth and development. Life is all about growth. It is one of the most viscerally fundamental of all human needs even though we do not always consciously recognize it. At any given moment we are either growing or retrogressing. If we are growing, we are achieving our purpose in life, and therefore we feel fulfilled. If we are retrogressing, we are moving away from our purpose and we feel empty and unfulfilled. Goals that we set ourselves are merely a tool for us to harness and direct our energies in service of our growth. They provide us with a means for organizing our lives and expressing our overall purpose. However, for the goals to be meaningful, the means we use to achieve those goals must be consistent with, as worthy, and as ennobling as the goals themselves. If we employ unworthy means, the goal itself becomes denuded of worth and meaning.

CHOOSING A NEW HABIT: A PRINCIPLED APPROACH TO ADDRESSING GLOBAL CHALLENGES

Once we have accepted that the means we use to tackle global challenges are just as important as the ends, we must shift the way we address these challenges. Given their complex and international nature, these challenges can only effectively be met with a system of global governance that is founded on a set of internationally accepted principles. At least a handful of trusted figures who have standing in the international community must identify these principles and lead other world leaders to ratify a global agreement to abide by them. It is imperative that all nations commit to weaving these principles into the structure of a new system of global governance and uncompromisingly applying these shared global ethics to solving challenges that arise.

Not only will these principles serve as necessary guideposts that can be used to extrapolate solutions to specific problems and responses to individual crises, but they will also be essential to shaping the global institutions discussed in the previous section. These principles must be woven into the very fabric of the new global institutions we build to ensure that they never succumb to the corruption and inefficacy that we witness today. Moreover, these principles will allow nations to think proactively, anticipating global challenges and preparing for them, rather than waiting for the crisis to occur and then reacting to it half-heartedly and only after inordinate delay. As our nations and global institutions act, they will be able to consider long-term consequences as well as short-term ones, while taking into account the interests of humanity as a whole, as opposed to narrowly-conceived national self-interest.

There is another reason to adopt this principled approach. Research has shown that individuals who mindfully adopt core values and live in accordance with them are far happier, more successful, and imbued with a greater sense that their lives have meaning than people whose behavior conflicts with their core values.[97] If humanity has become like a single organism, then our international behavior and the way nations treat other nations will produce the most constructive outcomes for humanity if they are aligned with a set of organizing principles on which we can all agree.

Another immense benefit that would flow from agreeing upon a set of shared principles is that the members of our international institutions would operate with a greater degree of comfort and confidence as they approach complex problems, making them more decisive in crafting solutions and more effective in their actions. They would no longer shirk making decisions or avoid action, nor would they feel that they were shooting in the dark. Rather, they would have the strength and determination that flow from knowing that they are following the spirit and letter of a clear mandate conferred upon them by the world's citizens, stamping their actions with unquestionable legitimacy.

By far the most compelling reason for adopting a set of global ethics is a truth that we introduced earlier in this work but that is worth repeating. Just as there are physical laws that govern our lives—such as the law of gravity—so, too are there principles that govern our social reality. The most important of these principles is the oneness of people and nations. These laws operate on us whether we choose to recognize and acknowledge them or not. However, let us be clear: We ignore them at our peril. Imagine what would happen if we were to build an airplane without taking into account the law of gravity. No one would want to fly in it, as the result would be disastrous! Why then, do we think when building institutions and organizations that govern our societies—whether political, social, financial, or otherwise—that we can ignore certain principles and truths about who we are as human beings and our relationship to each other without consequence? We flout these social realities at great cost to ourselves. It is no wonder that our social, economic, and political institutions are crumbling.

Fortunately, a number of prominent figures across various spheres of human activity have been preparing the ground for the adoption of a principled approach by talking about the importance of identifying and agreeing upon a shared set of foundational principles. One of these is Professor Kishore Mahbubani, whose analogy of the world as a vessel navigating stormy seas we partially discussed earlier in this work.[98] In addition to describing the world as a ship with 193 cabins, each of which has its own set rules and staff to govern its internal affairs yet lacking both captain and crew, he also observes that the governing rules being applied within some of these cabins pose a direct threat to the ship as a whole and may cause it to sink with all its occupants. Even prior to Professor Mahbubani's astute observation, the governing body of the Baha'i community in its 1985 message to the people of the world, titled "The Promise of World Peace," urged leaders to begin solving their problems by identifying the principles involved and then applying them, rather than turning to expedient solutions.[99]

Gareth Evans, former foreign minister of Australia and long-term head of the International Crisis Group similarly expressed his view that the only way to find viable and effective solutions to problems of governance was to first identify the principles involved and then apply them methodically. He bemoaned the fact that this was not current practice at any level of government that he had seen. Others who have joined the growing chorus calling for nations to make ethics a centerpiece of the debate on global governance and to adopt a set of core values and principles include well-regarded figures, such as Pascal Lamy, former director-general of the World Trade Organization,[100] and Ian Goldin, professor of Globalisation and Development at Oxford University.[101]

Learning From Our Past Successes

For those of you who are skeptical that it is possible for nations to agree on a set of global ethics, I would invite you to consider the universal adoption of a new principle, the "Responsibility to Protect" at the World Summit in New York in 2005. Although the application of this principle has been rocky as a result of the previously discussed inadequacies of the U.N., the process that was followed to achieve this goal is highly instructive and can be used as a roadmap to replicate a similar success in achieving global consensus around a set of shared global ethics. The principle was first introduced in 2001 by the International Commission on Intervention and State Sovereignty, a body created by the Canadian government at the turn of the century and tasked

with examining new ways of addressing the complex problem that arises when the people of a country suffer human
rights abuses at the hands of their government either
because of the inability or the unwillingness of that government to protect them.

The first step the Commission took was to carefully consider the language to employ in framing the conversation.
It avoided controversial language such as the "right to intervene," which had been used in the past but had elicited
strong adverse responses because of its association with
colonialist aspirations and with attempts to interfere with
perceived rights enshrined in state sovereignty. Instead, the
Commission adopted new language to articulate a "responsibility to protect," under which the international community is ultimately responsible to protect people suffering
from serious and irreparable harm, such as large-scale loss of
life and gross human rights atrocities, and people who are
in dire need of protection if their own government cannot
or will not protect them. By using new language, the Commission evoked the noble human sentiments of responsibility and protection and called for governments and leaders
to rethink their previously entrenched positions as individual nations and as members of a community of nations.

The Commission offered this newly articulated principle
as one around which the international community could
build consensus.[102] It was successful in achieving its goal.
This principle was endorsed by the U.N. Secretary General[103] and ultimately by all the world leaders at the World
Summit that marked the beginning of the 21st century in
September 2005.[104] Although the R2P doctrine has been,
at best, ineffectively implemented, the fundamental step of
nations coming together in agreement on a set of shared

principles was a profound precedent for future international acceptance of global ethics. Unfortunately, the international structures in place at the time of R2P's introduction were inherently incapable of adequately supporting and enforcing the doctrine, however, future institutions of global governance can and should have the strength to properly implement such crucial international decisions.

Similarly, although the U.N. is no longer up to task in handling the complex problems with which it is faced, the inception of the United Nations system was groundbreaking and exemplary in its foundation on a set of principles, articulated and agreed upon by Prime Minister Churchill and President Roosevelt in the Atlantic Charter. The Charter was a declaration that resulted from a meeting between Winston Churchill and Franklin Roosevelt on board a naval vessel off the coast of Newfoundland in August 1941. In it the two leaders set out their purpose, saying they "deem it right to make known certain common principles in the national policies of their respective countries on which they base their hopes for a better future of the world."[105] The Charter contained eight common principles and was the basis for the creation of the United Nations.

A new international security system better equipped to serve global interests in the 21st century can be created on a comparable basis of global ethics. A core group of leaders must draw up a statement of such principles and labor untiringly to obtain the wholehearted commitment of their fellow leaders. This statement should include at the minimum the following principles that reflect the growth of humanity and meet its needs as it stands at the threshold of its maturity.

The Oneness of Nations and Peoples

This principle is the foundation of all others and should be made the chief operating principle of international relations. All other core values must be tested against and found congruent with it. It serves as the glue that binds together all other principles and values the leaders agree upon and ensures the integrity of the foundation as a whole. It must be the driving moral force that influences and shapes all other values, policies, laws, and institutional infrastructure that are crafted to ensure universal peace and collective security. Starting from the premise that we are all one would alone give us the clarity to identify organic changes that we need to make to our current laws, policies, procedures and institutions while ensuring that new institutions and procedures are built on foundations that ensure our long-term well-being.

A brief example will serve to illustrate this idea. It would be unthinkable to have a new international executive, the international organization primarily tasked with maintaining the world's peace and security, operating on the basis that a handful of nations possess the power to veto decisions that would conduce to the long-term peace and security of all, as is the case today with the Security Council of the United Nations. It would also be unthinkable that a few nations should have the privilege of permanent members on such a body—as is also currently the case on the Security Council—while others were somehow considered second-class global citizens and deprived of such a privilege.

Justice and Equity

All nations and peoples must be treated justly and fairly, without favor or discrimination. Several consequences follow from this. One is that certain key resources must be shared fairly. For example, provisions must be made and international mechanisms set up to allow all nations and peoples equal and fair access to critical sources of energy such as oil, water, and nuclear power. As we negotiate the treacherous waters of a pandemic, we are learning how important it is that all people also have equitable access to personal protective equipment and life-saving equipment like ventilators. In addition, it is imperative that all nations be able to obtain access to any medicines or vaccines that are developed to treat or prevent infection from the virus.

Another consequence that should flow from the application of these principles is that crises and threats that affect different peoples and nations should be accorded the same importance regardless of whether they involve wealthy or poor nations, powerful or weak ones. For example, the international community should respond to the types of human rights atrocities that occurred in Rwanda and Darfur with the same alacrity that it did to the September 11, 2001 attacks in New York City. It should also respond equally to the threat of a pandemic such as COVID-19, whether the pandemic is raging in Asia, Europe, North America, or Africa. This sense of fairness can only stem from an understanding of our interconnectedness and oneness. If one part of the international body politic is suffering, then the entire body must rally to its protection and defence.

One of the consequences of applying the principles of justice and equity will be that rules embodying what behaviors are acceptable and unacceptable by nations must be clearly spelled out in advance and made known to all, along with the specific punishments that will result from their breach. These rules must then be applied consistently and equally with respect to all nations, regardless of the identity of the offending nation. Similarly, punishments must be meted out even-handedly to all offenders. In other words, we can no longer condone or tolerate the practice of double standards. It follows that breaches of the rules on the non-proliferation of nuclear weapons must be punished equally, whether the offending party is a nation that is powerful and well-liked in the international community or weak and unpopular.

Similarly, all nations should be required to open their doors for unlimited international inspection if called upon to do so, regardless of their status as friend or perceived foe of states serving on decision-making institutions. Illegal occupation of territory must be dealt with equally, regardless of the nation engaging in the unlawful behavior or the perceived importance of the victim nation to others in the international community. All borders must be sacrosanct, protected from wilful violation by the collective might of the world community. Finally, rules affecting international peace and security should apply to all nations if a critical majority (to be defined by our leaders) of the world's nations support their creation. So, for example, all treaties involving human rights issues, such as torture, the status of women, or the civil and political rights of people, as well as treaties involving non-proliferation issues and treaties creating international organizations such as the International

Criminal Court, should be binding upon all nations without exception. No nation should be given the choice of opting out, as this compromises the integrity of the system's fabric and eventually causes it to unravel.

The importance of the principles of justice and equity cannot be overstated. Their faithful and widespread application will eventually dissipate suspicion and feelings of injustice among nations and peoples of the world. They will also be a central element of a transparent system in which all players are held equally accountable. As a consequence, an atmosphere of trust amongst nations and peoples will be engendered, which is essential for building a peaceful and secure world in which all nations are eventually unified.

Collective Action in the Collective Interest

Another powerful principle is that the advantage of the part is best reached by ensuring the advantage of the whole, and that there can be no long-term benefit for a component part if the interests of the whole are neglected. The only way a nation can assure its own self-interest is by working assiduously for the collective interest of all nations.

This was the lesson that the countries of Western Europe learned in the aftermath of World War II. Decimated and crushed as their infrastructure, economies and societies were, the countries of Europe all sought coal and steel on equal terms to rebuild themselves. They also wanted to ensure that advantageous access to coal and steel did not allow Germany to initiate another war. The solution they ultimately agreed upon was to pool their coal and steel resources under the management of a supranational High Authority that was given expansive powers to ensure that each member country had access to the coal and steel it needed on fair terms, and that all production and sales of these materials were transparent to all. The common market for coal and steel that was thus born was known as the European Coal and Steel Community (ECSC).

Significantly, the nations that formed this new community joined only after long debate and analysis led each party to conclude, in its particular political, economic, and historical situation, that its interests would be served better by acting with other nations for the collective interest of all the members, than by working alone. It is also significant that, having understood this fundamental principle, each of the six founding member nations willingly gave up some sovereignty over these two critical resources—the functional equivalents of oil and gas for us today—to a supranational agency that worked for the collective interests of all. Most crucially, the creation of an institution based on the principle of the need to work for the collective advantage, as well as other principles identified above, brought peace to Europe after centuries of intermittent wars, and was the first step in the gradual evolution of what we know today as the European Union, a union that currently embraces twenty-seven European states within its ambit.

During this period of the COVID-19 pandemic, it is interesting to observe the glimmerings of dawning recognition within nations that the first three principles are at work in our interconnected world and should be more consciously brought to bear in our decisions and relationships. Two particular examples are illustrative of this development.

The first involves a proposal advanced by President Emmanuel Macron of France and Chancellor Angela Merkel of Germany that reflected a radical shift by Germany away from its historical aversion to sharing financial burdens with other European Union members. The proposal was for the European Union to borrow hundreds of billion euros on behalf of all the E.U. members to establish a recovery fund for helping member countries most affected by the coronavirus. As eventually adopted by the European Union in July 2020, just over half of this help to countries hardest hit will be in the form of grants with no obligation of repayment, with the rest to come in the form of loans.[106] For the first time ever, the E.U. will take on a vast, common debt in the name of the European Union as a whole, using the collective body's excellent credit standing, and, further, will take on financial responsibility to pay about half of it—potentially through common taxes—policies that Germany has traditionally opposed. In addition, the plan contemplates transferring funds from richer countries to support poorer ones, another policy that Germany has traditionally rejected. Each of these behaviors represents a complete shift away from Germany's previous fiscal positions.[107]

In making this change, the German Chancellor is choosing to put the interests of the 27-nation bloc before Germany's national interests. The move is based on an understanding that the economic havoc that is being wreaked by the coronavirus will not only damage the poorer nations of Southern Europe, but it will also damage the wealthier northern nations such as France and Germany who rely on their southern relations to provide both labor and consumption of their goods, both of which are indispensable to the north's survival. Their decision is based on a growing understanding that the principles of oneness apply, that their national advantage can only be assured by ensuring the advantage of the European Union as a whole, and that justice and equity dictate that their policies shift. As President of the European Commission, President Ursula von der Leyen said, "This is about all of us and it is way bigger than any of us."[108]

While the deal also includes components that are driven by expediency in a bid to get the agreement of some Central European countries like Hungary, it is nevertheless remarkable in the aspects discussed here. This event provides us with a greater understanding of the interplay between the adoption of a core set of values and foundational principles and the creation of institutions of governance that must be based on these principles and reflect them in its structures and processes. In this case, the understanding of the principles has led the European Union to propose a step, which, if taken, will move the union closer in the direction of its founding father, Jean Monnet's vision, of a federated Europe. As explored in more depth in my previous book, *Bridge to Global Governance*, Jean Monnet hoped that the European project he devised resulting in today's European Union would achieve ever-deepening integration over time. He likened this process to adding links progressively to a chain of European integration.[109]

Limit National Sovereignty While Avoiding Excessive Centralization

A principle that goes hand in hand with the need to replace our collective habit of nationalism with the development of a new system of collective governance is the principle of limiting national sovereignty while avoiding excessive centralization. National sovereignty must be limited to the extent necessary to protect the citizens of the world as a whole against climate change, global pandemics, nuclear proliferation, or economic collapse. The willingness to adopt this principle will depend in large part on a deep understanding that the advantage of the part is assured if we bend all our energies to ensuring the advantage of the whole. This principle demands that all national impulses be subordinated to the requirements of a unified world.

Although this principle requires that all nations be willing to cede control over certain important powers they possess in areas where collective action serves their interests better than individual action, it does not aim to do away with nation states. Rather, it recognizes that these states serve a useful function as distinct, identifiable entities responsible for the welfare and protection of their people, and accountable to them and to the international community for any failure to discharge this weighty responsibility. Nor does it aim to snuff out the kind of intelligent patriotism that motivates citizens of each country to contribute to the advancement of the arts, sciences, education, health, and general welfare of their country, or seek to impose a unity based on uniformity. On the contrary, it is important that nation states continue to exercise authority and power in certain domains to avoid the dangers of excessive centralization on the one hand, while also encouraging and maintaining diversity within the context of a new and unified system of global governance on the other.

Using Force in Service of Justice

This principle requires that we accept the reality that humanity has not yet achieved a degree of maturity that allows it to dispense with the use of force altogether. However, its use must be severely limited and regulated. It must be used only after a collective decision is made by institutions of global governance representing all nations and people of the world—such as an international executive as discussed above—based on collectively-agreed rules made by a world parliament, and by a force that represents all the nations of the world, namely an international standing force. In other words, at this stage in our collective development there will still be times when war becomes a strong basis upon which to build peace, and ruin a pathway to reconstruction.

There are occasions when war is waged for a righteous purpose, for instance when it becomes necessary to remove a genocidal leader. In such an instance one can view the use of force as an instrument of justice that is necessary to restore peace just as one might use chemotherapy to ensure the health and survival of a cancer patient. According to Gareth Evans, the idea that "war can be a progressive cause," and that military intervention is in certain circumstances "not merely defensible, but a compelling obligation" is one that the international community had to relearn in the 1990s.[110] Michael Levi and Michael O'Hanlon, two scholars at the Brookings Institution, support this principle as well. In their book *The Future of Arms Control* they say that "there may now be situations in which, paradoxically, war in the near term is preferable to an illusory peace."[111]

The ability to use timely and adequate force is a critical element in the creation of a strong and effective system of global governance that can ensure peace and collective security. Such a system demands both strength and elasticity. Its strength depends on having the military and police forces necessary to quell disturbances to international peace and security at the international community's beck and call. However, the system will only work if the threat of the use of force is a credible one. Thus, it is evident that this principle is intimately connected to the proposal discussed above to establish a strong international executive backed by a robust international standing force.

An example of the threat of force as a tool to goad countries into complying with edicts of an international agency involves Iraq in 2002. In August 1990 Iraqi President Saddam Hussein illegally invaded Kuwait and defied calls from the international community, including a Security Council resolution, to withdraw his forces from Iraq. Consequently, an international coalition formed under the authority of Security Council Resolution 678, led by the United States, and consisting of 35 countries, forced Iraq to withdraw from Kuwait. This interference resulted in the first Gulf War, which lasted from August 1990 to the end of February 1991.

The coalition was successful in forcing Iraq to leave Kuwait. Under the peace terms Iraq not only agreed to recognize Kuwait but to also get rid of its weapons of mass destruction, including nuclear weapons. Over the following years, Iraq made many efforts to interfere with the work of the U.N. weapons inspectors. This ultimately led to Iraq's firm refusal in 1998 to admit weapons inspectors into the country to do their job. In the summer of 2002 the U.S. and Britain began to build up a military force in anticipation of possible action against Iraq if it continued to defy Security Council resolutions calling on it to comply with its disarmament commitments and allow weapons inspections to resume their work. On September 16, 2002 Iraq unconditionally agreed to the return of inspectors.[112] According to Hans Blix, former director general of the International Atomic Energy Agency, and later the Executive Chairman of the United Nations Monitoring, Verification and Inspection Commission, the "essential reason"' why Iraq accepted the inspectors back was the credible threat of force from the British and American militaries.[113]

The exercise of flexibility and restraint in deciding when to use force lends the system some elasticity and should be reflected both in the rules that specify the circumstances in which action is to be taken, and in the judgment of the institutions tasked with applying those rules. The growing acceptance by the international community over the course of the past fifteen years of the Responsibility to Protect, an obligation to protect people within a country's boundaries—that falls initially on the shoulders of the state in question, and only by default upon the international community itself—is an example of the exercise of such flexibility and restraint when crafting rules for the protection of the peoples of the world.

Collective Security

This principle requires that all nations must come to an agreement that is designed to guarantee international peace and security and that specifies all the requirements necessary to achieve this goal. It might be sensible for a handful of leaders who have a global reputation for trustworthiness, high-mindedness, and good intentions to serve the best interests of all of humanity to come together to begin the process. Once they have reached agreement they can then seek to have their fellow leaders ratify it. Under this agreement they commit themselves to limit the amounts of arms they each possess to the minimum amount required to preserve peace and order within their borders. Any additional arms must be destroyed under the supervision of a world parliament, as discussed above. They must also agree that if a nation takes any action that threatens or breaches the terms of the international agreement on peace and security, they will all arise as one to bring down that government and replace it with one that can work as a peaceful member of the community of nations. To achieve this, the community of nations must have an international standing force at its disposal.

Global Ethics Must Shape the Structure and Operation of Global Governance Institutions

It is evident from our exploration of the new proposed habit of building institutions of global governance to replace nationalism, and the further proposed habit of identifying a system of global ethics to replace expediency, that there is an interplay and inextricable connection between the two. Indeed, the latter must be woven into the very fabric of the former in order for the new proposed system of global governance to effectively and viably serve the well-being and best interests of humanity.

OLD MINDSET 6: WE CANNOT TRUST PEOPLE IN POSITIONS OF AUTHORITY

One of the features of modern-day society is the prevalent belief that we cannot trust our leaders to properly serve us, whether at the local, national, regional, or international level. Indeed, trust in public institutions has plummeted to an all-time low. Our leaders have a seemingly insatiable appetite for power, which they view as a limited commodity. They are intensely competitive in their pursuit of it and they are willing to do almost anything to acquire it. They use their power as an instrument of control and domination over the people they are supposed to represent and the resources that they are supposed to use to serve the well-being of those people. Through their repeated abuse of power, we have been conditioned to believe that people in authority are likely to misuse their position to amass power and influence, which they in turn use to further their own private interests at the expense of those whom they purportedly represent. As a result, we feel entitled to be cynical about what our politicians say and do. We often operate on the assumption that they lie to us, and we even expect them to do so.

One of the unfortunate consequences of this mindset is that we feel powerless to change this state of affairs. As a result, many of us abdicate our individual responsibility to elect worthy and deserving leaders who possess the qualities of integrity and unselfish motives, and who have demonstrated records of selfless service. We either fail to vote or do not bother taking the time to properly investigate the character, motivations, and record of service of candidates for leadership positions. In relinquishing these rights and privileges, we are unwittingly complicit in perpetuating the same corrupt and unworthy systems of government that repeatedly fail to meet the needs of their people.

OLD HABIT OF ELECTING UNFIT LEADERS

The central reason why we end up with such unworthy leaders is that we elect them without proper regard to three essential criteria: their qualities of character, their motivations in seeking office, and their demonstrated record of service. Consequently, we often find ourselves with leaders and governments who abjectly fail in their responsibility to ensure the welfare of the people they must serve, and who create new problems that further erode the fabric of their nations. We need look no further than our leaders' response to climate change and the COVID-19 pandemic as proof of this reality. In both instances, despite repeated warnings about disasters that lay ahead, many leaders around the world failed to take adequate steps to plan and prepare. When they acted, they did too little, too late, and they continue to deny reality and procrastinate even as evidence of the disasters resulting from these twin crises accumulates daily.

Another glaring example of a government's abject failure to tend to the needs of its people was the explosion of 2,750 tons of high-density ammonium nitrate in the port of Beirut in August 2020. The blast was the equivalent of a 3.3 magnitude earthquake and was so strong that it was felt as far away as Cyprus—125 miles away.[114] The damage to life and property was horrendous, with at least 190 people dead, over 6,500 injured, and major damage to over half of the city of Beirut, amounting to at least $15 billion dollars and leaving hundreds of thousands of people without homes. Two of the city's hospitals were so badly damaged that they had to close their doors.[115]

All of this pain and suffering was entirely avoidable. The ammonium nitrate that caused the blast had been stored in a warehouse at the port for about seven years, starting in 2013. Everyone from the customs officials who were storing it to the judicial authorities whose responsibility it was to decide how to safely store and dispose of it knew that the conditions under which it was stored were likely to lead to a massive explosion. According to official records, the port authority had written to the judicial authorities on the matter several times, begging them to make a decision about its safe storage and disposition, to no avail.[116]

The level of incompetence, mismanagement, and negligence that resulted in the untold losses to life and property are inexcusable. Unfortunately, this tragedy is only the most recent evidence of the damage that is wrought in a country in which so much energy is devoted to dividing power among eighteen religious sects, resulting in a long-established pattern of political deadlock and paralysis.

We desperately lack the leadership we need and deserve, not only at the national level, but also at the international scale. We were forcefully reminded of this fact when the U.N. Secretary-General António Guterres called for a global ceasefire in order to marshall all efforts to fight COVID-19. Instead of rallying to this call for global solidarity in the face of a deadly common enemy by passing a ceasefire resolution, three of the permanent members of the U.N. Security Council—the United States, Russia, and China—blocked its passage. As an editorial column in *The Guardian* reported, "This pathetic inability on the part of the world's great powers to show leadership, compassion and common sense at a time of global emergency is dangerous and disheartening."[117]

Characteristics of Unfit Leaders

It is worth exploring some of the serious character flaws that render such leaders unfit to meet the needs of their people or to address the multiplying challenges—both national and global—of our time.

CORRUPTION

The first is corruption. Alas, examples in which elected leaders and politicians have become mired in corruption scandals abound. In 2018 the government of Mariano Rajoy in Spain fell because it was found to have been operating an illegal slush fund.[118] In Brazil, another massive corruption scandal, which came to be known as "Operation Car Wash," led to corruption probes starting in 2014 and ending in prison sentences for many politicians and executives. It implicated President Michel Temer and former President Dilma Rousseff, and it resulted in a prison sentence for former President Luiz Lula da Silva. It ultimately paved the way for the populist government of Jair Bolsanaro to sweep into power on an anti-corruption platform. The scandal centered on the state-owned oil company Petrobras that was suspected of accepting bribes from companies in return for contracts. The investigation resulted in over two hundred convictions for crimes that included money laundering, drug trafficking, and corruption. The scandal had many tentacles that caused the leaders of several other countries including Colombia, Peru, and Venezuela to be implicated.[119]

Meanwhile, in spring 2017 South Korean president Park Geun-hye was impeached by South Korea's parliament and ousted on charges of bribery and abuse of presidential power. She was later convicted of bribery, extortion, abuse of power, and other criminal charges and was given large fines and a twenty-five year prison sentence. The case exposed a corrupt system of collusive ties between the chaebol—family controlled conglomerates—and South Korean politicians.[120]

Similarly, a culture of corruption at the top political levels became increasingly evident in South Africa in the 2010s. Despite promises by the ruling African National Congress to provide a good education for Black citizens, millions of dollars allocated for education were misspent and disappeared into the pockets of corrupt politicians, resulting in school facilities that are not fit because of leaky roofs, lack of water, collapsing retaining walls, and toilets so unsafe that they lead to deaths. Children all too often have to use pit toilets that are unsafe and prone to collapse, swallowing them up and causing them to drown.[121]

During the last elections for the French presidency in 2017, François Fillon, who was projected to win, and who had served as Prime Minister under President Nicolas Sarkozy was forced to step aside when he was accused of creating fake jobs for his wife and two children, thereby unlawfully enriching himself and his family at the expense of taxpayers. Not only did Mr. Fillon lose his reputation and an opportunity to serve his country as president, but he and his wife were also ultimately tried and found guilty of embezzling one million euros in supposed payments for the non-existent jobs as his parliamentary assistants. The couple was sentenced by a French court in June 2020. Mr. Fillon received a five year jail sentence, three of which were suspended. His wife received a three year suspended sentence.[122]

PREJUDICE

The second character flaw of our leaders that has led to egregious human rights abuses and perpetuation of deep injustices is prejudice. The immense suffering of the people of Syria stems not only from the desire of an authoritarian dictator to quell the demands of the people for more freedom, but also from sectarian prejudice that pits the leadership's Shia Alawite sect against a Sunni Muslim majority. The resulting almost decade-long civil war has, to date, caused at least 367,965 reported deaths and 192,035 people reported missing and presumed dead. In addition, more than half of the Syrian population has been uprooted, with at least 6.2 million Syrians internally displaced, and close to another 6 million fleeing as refugees to neighboring countries and beyond.[123]

The discriminatory policies of Myanmar's Buddhist government aimed at the minority Rohingya Muslim community, coupled with the government's persecution of that community is another example of the impact that prejudice at the level of government has on its victims. While this prejudice has been evident since the late 1970s, it manifested itself in aggravated form in 2017 with renewed violence that included murder, rape and arson. Consequently, a large contingent of Rohingya Muslims fled Myanmar, with a large number taking refuge in Bangladesh where they live in difficult conditions in massive refugee camps along the border of the two countries.[124]

The Indian government has recently made several decisions that mark a shift from the secular society founded by Mr. Nehru when India gained its independence to a more sectarian Hindu one. Each of the three decisions effectively results in discrimination against the Muslim minority. The first was the decision in August 2019 to abruptly revoke the limited autonomy that had been granted to Jammu and Kashmir under Article 370 of India's Constitution. The territory has now been split into two parts, Jammu and

Kashmir, and Ladakh, both of which are now under Indian federal control.[125]

The second decision was the Citizenship Amendment Act passed in December 2019 that allows members of six minority religious communities, namely Hindus, Sikhs, Parsis, Buddhists, Jains, and Christians, to apply for citizenship on a fast track, but that excludes Muslims.[126] The latest action was one made by the Indian Supreme Court granting Hindus in Ayodhya the right to ownership of a site that had, until recently, been home to a mosque. The site had been at the center of disputes over ownership between Hindus and Muslims over several decades.[127] Several months after the decision, in August 2020, the Indian Prime Minister, Mr. Modi, participated in a ceremony in which he laid the cornerstone for a Hindu Temple to be built on the site of what had been the mosque in Ayodhya. This site has since been the scene of many violent sectarian clashes between Hindus and Muslims.[128] All three decisions separately and in combination discriminate against the Muslim minority and corrode the fabric of Indian society by exacerbating the sectarian tensions between Hindus and Muslims.

Another example of note is the religious prejudice that has led the Shiite government of Iran to persecute the Baha'i minority ever since that government came into power in 1979. The persecution has been systematic and has put the Baha'is under intense pressure. The government's avowed goal, as reflected in a secret memorandum written by the Supreme Revolutionary Cultural Council in 1991, has been essentially to quietly annihilate the Baha'i community in Iran.[129] Since then, Baha'is have been imprisoned, tortured, and killed. Baha'i students are barred from attending university, and those who have worked to support the Baha'i Institute for Higher Education in a volunteer capacity are in danger of harassment, arrest, and imprisonment. Baha'is are also denied jobs and business licenses, their businesses are shut down, and their lawful pensions and inheritances denied. Baha'i properties are confiscated and destroyed, their cemeteries are desecrated, the faith's leadership imprisoned, and rights to assemble and worship severely curtailed.[130] Time and again the Baha'is have been promised their freedom if only they will recant their faith and convert to Islam.[131]

The structural barriers and systemic unjust treatment of people of color in the United States also reflects prejudice and malice on the part of leadership. Evidence abounds that people of color, in particular the Black community, face an uphill struggle in obtaining adequate housing, education, healthcare, and employment, due to historical and continued white supremacy and anti-Black racism in U.S. systems and culture.[132] Moreover, there are too many instances of Black individuals being regularly and systematically targeted and abused by law enforcement authorities, who have demonstrated a pattern of stopping, arresting, and treating them with unwarranted and inhumane brutality, resulting in tragic deaths. In summer 2020, after another series of police killings and brutality against Black people, protests broke out in hundreds of U.S. cities. People took to the streets to demand revolutionary change in these racist systems, and to call for justice for Black individuals whose lives have been affected by police brutality. Despite curfews, the activation of the National Guard in many cities, and continued brutality against protesters, widespread protests have persisted for months.[133]

DISHONESTY

A third character flaw in leaders that is a serious hindrance to proper governance is dishonesty. Unfortunately, this shortcoming has been so prevalent for such a long period of time that many of us have come to expect that our politicians and elected leaders will lie to us. What is confounding and dismaying is that we have become numb to it and accepted it. Our complacency has only contributed to an exacerbation of this problem. In a world that is so fraught with risk such as the risk of nuclear war, blatant dishonesty on the part of our leaders is positively dangerous. The degree and scale of political lies was highlighted by the April 3 2017 issue of *Time Magazine,* whose dramatic cover posited the question, "Is Truth Dead?" Various iterations of this question have surfaced again and again in media and academia, demonstrating the growing and increasingly urgent discourse on the importance of truth-telling and honesty from people in positions of power.[134]

It is time we woke up and accepted that we reap what we sow. If an electoral candidate has demonstrated that they are unable or unwilling to be faithful to their spouse and their children, why should we believe that they will magically transform and be honest to us once they are elected? Similarly, if a person has demonstrated a willingness to behave dishonestly and cheat in their business dealings, why should we expect them to behave any differently once they are in power? Rather, we should understand that their perspective on life is that the ends justify the means. So long as they get the power they seek, then it doesn't matter if they have to lie to get there—including making promises that they have no intention or ability to keep.

INCOMPETENCE

A fourth hindrance to good governance is electing leaders who lack the administrative skills, wisdom, knowledge of statecraft, and understanding of foreign relations and domestic relations necessary to fulfill their duties competently. Without these skills that constitute basic competence, an elected leader is not only ill-equipped to discharge their duties to ensure the well-being of their citizens, but is also likely to unwittingly make decisions and take actions that actively undermine that well-being. An example that comes to mind is what happens when we elect leaders who are ignorant of the realities of climate change, including the disastrous consequences it will have on all aspects of human life in every single part of the world, and who therefore fail to take the necessary steps to arrest it or to mitigate its effects.[135]

LACK OF COURAGE

Another key character flaw is lack of courage. What we must look for and what we deserve to find in our leaders are qualities of commitment and courage. In other words, we must endeavor to elect leaders who are willing to do what is right and necessary even though it means wading into uncharted territory. Their courage must manifest itself in a number of key ways. They must not be worried about whether their decisions and actions are popular or not; they must simply want to do what they believe is right and what will benefit their people. These are the kinds of leaders that exercise their creativity to come up with innovative solutions to complex problems. These are the kinds of leaders we so need in this day when we are faced with seemingly intractable global challenges like climate change, a global pandemic, and a global economic recession the likes of which we have never yet experienced. If we are to arrive at a goal of zero net carbon emissions by 2050, we need to have leaders who are courageous and willing to do what no one before them has dared to do to secure the survival and well-being of humanity.

This kind of courage also requires that our leaders are willing to tell us the truth about fixes we are in and what it will take for us to get out of them. This quality is extremely rare in our leaders who fear that telling us the harsh truth about what we need to do to mitigate global warming or solve other global challenges will cost them the next election. Consequently, they prefer to fudge the issues, or better yet deflect, ignore and avoid them, and if necessary lie. A blunt quotation attributed to Jean-Claude Juncker when he was Prime Minister of Luxembourg (later President of the European Union) states the problem: "We all know what to do, we just don't know how to get re-elected after we've done it."[136]

This statement represents so much of what is wrong with the attitude of our leaders, starting with the fact that they have come to believe that their primary role as leaders is to ensure that they can maintain their positions and powers. Instead of thinking how they can best serve the people who have entrusted them with the sacred responsibility of ensuring their well-being, they are thinking of what they can do or avoid doing to ensure that they are re-elected. They are willing to barter away the interests of their people for their own personal interest. This brings us full circle back to the importance of adjusting our old mindset regarding our relationship with those in authority to understand that the reason why our leaders are elected is to create the necessary conditions for all of us to thrive and to fulfill our individual and collective potential. They are in positions of service to their people, rather than in positions to enable them to feather their own nests.

In her address to government officials, business leaders, and civil society leaders at the opening of the United Nations Climate Summit held in New York in September 2019, the young climate activist Greta Thunberg chided the international representatives for failing the next generation, spinning fairy tales about unending economic growth and lacking the maturity to "tell it like it is."[137]

The point she was attempting to drive home is that we expect leaders to have the courage to tell us the truth about the situations that we encounter, about the dangers we face, and about the opportunities that are before us. They need to be willing to tell us the uncomfortable truth about the sacrifices we will need to make to arrest and mitigate climate change so that we do not destroy ourselves and our way of life completely. A failure to be forthright and courageous in telling things as they are sorely underestimates people's capacity to grasp and accept reality and take opportunities to do the right thing individually and as communities. For this to happen, leaders must be willing to give us unalloyed facts, present innovative solutions that are manifestly in the collective interest, and invite their people to partner with them in implementing these solutions.

Motives and Record of Service

In addition to the fact that we lack the habit of looking for certain qualities that are crucial to good leadership, we also have the destructive habit of relying on the words and promises of people who seek to be leaders rather than examining their motives and their record of service when assessing their fitness for office.

One of the key motives that we must look for is wanting and being willing to work for the collective interest rather than the individual's personal interest. In today's world with the easy access that so many of us have to information it is not hard to discern these motives by examining the candidate's past record of service. Their actions reveal whether their motives and intentions are selfless and sincere and whether they reflect a willingness to sacrifice their own good for that of their community. Have they been willing to forget their own worldly advantage in order to advance the common good, or have they been prone to pursuing their personal interest, seeking adulation, self-aggrandizement and material enrichment at the expense of others? During general elections held in countries as far apart and seemingly different as South Korea, Venezuela, the United States, and South Africa, it was striking to hear a common refrain among ordinary people interviewed in the streets: that they hoped the leaders who were ultimately elected would work to serve the interests of their people rather than to advance their own self-interest.

The failure of leaders at the national and global levels to adequately prepare their nations and the world for the onslaught of the COVID-19 pandemic despite years of warning that a pandemic was coming is a glaring example of two things. The first was a failure of imagination of the scale and devastation of a pandemic. The second was an unwillingness to do what it took, including spending money and harnessing political will to prepare for a pandemic despite these warnings because they believed it was unlikely to happen on their watch. Instead of being motivated to act and do the right thing to protect their populations, they chose instead to put their own interests first and desist from doing something that they feared would cost them the next election.

One of the unsavory and destructive features of our current systems of elections in most parts of the world is the inordinate influence that moneyed interests play in determining who gets elected. Systems of election in which political candidates rely on contributions to support their elections inevitably result in the successful candidate feeling beholden to those who paid to get them elected and bound to make decisions that benefit those interests first and foremost, even if these interests conflict with the interests of the general population. Such systems are manifestly unfair and represent a form of corruption that has been institutionalized for so long that it has become widely accepted. Indeed, according to *The Economist* magazine, studies show that, "[a]s inequality increases so does the political influence of the rich." Moreover, in the United States alone, apparently "fewer than 30,000 people account for a quarter of all national political donations from individuals and for more than 80% of the money raised by political parties."[138] These figures demonstrate the bankruptcy of our system of government in which a small handful of individuals have such a massive and disproportionate influence in who gets elected and the decisions they make.

Our entrenched habit of electing unfit leaders has led us to a world fraught with corruption, polarization, and disenchantment with our systems of governance. As our apathy and disengagement with government grows, we cede further ground to corrupt and power-hungry leaders who are only too happy to take advantage of any opportunity to seize power and control over our lives and our resources to aggrandize themselves and satisfy their own self-interest. One of the most harmful results that flows from this negative cycle is the polarization and disunity it causes in our communities, whether local, national, or international. Without unity, society fragments and our problems only multiply.

ACCEPTING THAT POWER RESIDES IN THE PEOPLE

However, the real threat is less about the weight of unbearably corrupt institutions and leaders, rather it is more rooted in our perception of the role we play in perpetuating this painfully ineffective system. Instead of viewing elected leaders and governments as figures with endless authority who impose their selfish interests on us, we can choose to recognize our power and agency in electing these leaders. We are not at the mercy of leaders who are inept and self-serving. In fact, we have the immense privilege and task of actively engaging in electing people who we believe are best suited to the task of ensuring our well-being and tending to our collective interest. Naturally, this agency is more readily accessible in democratic systems, however, the kernel of truth still remains that more power resides within the masses than in small clusters of corrupt leadership. With this privilege comes the responsibility to choose our leaders wisely, based on an assessment of their character, motivations, and record of service as discussed above. We have the capacity to mobilize and change our systems of governance to better serve our needs.

REFRAMING OUR MINDSET:
THE LEADERSHIP SHIFT

If we replaced our cynical views of authority with more empowering and constructive ones, and if we regarded their role as essential to maintaining social order and ensuring that communities are well-organized and that all legitimate social needs are consistently and fairly assessed and met, we would likely feel far more enthusiastic about our leaders and institutions of governance. Such a view of the critical role leadership plays would energize and motivate us to find suitable candidates to fill positions of authority. We would view our ability to vote as a sacred privilege, and we would accept full responsibility for the quality of leaders we elect. If we regarded the primary task of our leaders and institutions as enabling, encouraging, and guiding the people they serve, with the ultimate goal of creating the conditions necessary for us to fulfill our individual and collective potential, and if we elected leaders who truly committed to this responsibility, we would repose our trust in leaders far more readily.

A useful analogy to consider in understanding the essential role of leaders in maintaining a healthy system of social organization is that of a school. In every school there is a basic hierarchy in which the principal and the administration are tasked with the responsibility to set the standards, curricula, vision, and goals of the school. The faculty and other members of staff set about executing that vision and the students play their role in following the guidance and instruction and putting forth their best effort to learn. Each group has its part to play in ensuring that the school's purpose—the proper moral, intellectual, and physical education of students—is best met. A school in which faculty members are suspicious of the motives, character, or competence of the principal and administration is one in which neither faculty nor students thrive. Similarly, if the students suspect that their teachers are simply there to collect a paycheck and do not care about the development of the students, then the students will not thrive. If the students do not believe their teachers have the capacity to adequately teach, they will not afford them their due respect, nor will they take their guidance and instructions seriously. This lack of trust will undermine the very purpose of the school.

Ultimately, adopting a new vision of what we seek and demand in a true leader, someone who the American entrepreneur and motivational speaker Jim Rohn so aptly observed helps others shift their "thoughts, beliefs, and actions for the better,"[139] will enable us to move from an experience marked by dictatorial authority to one resulting in the empowerment of the community driven by frank and respectful consultation that seeks to arrive at truths that benefit the wider interests of the community as a whole. In addition, the role of such a leader is to raise the consciousness of the people and lead them to unity of thought and action based on accurate information and evolving collective understanding and insight.

Responsibility to Educate Public Opinion

One of our dysfunctional societal habits is our tendency to make certain decisions and engage in certain behaviors that have far-reaching consequences on our well-being without the benefit of adequate information. Consequently, we act in ignorance about the dangers that face us, the scope of opportunities and alternative courses of action that are available to us, and the likely consequences of our decisions and actions. This destructive habit is inextricably bound with and a consequence of the habit we have just discussed, of electing unfit leaders who are unwilling to give us the relevant facts that affect our well-being because they are attached to power and they fear that we will punish them by removing them from office.

It is worth examining a couple of instances in relatively recent history when our leaders have actually risen to the occasion and made the effort to educate public opinion about the consequences of taking a proposed course of action versus the consequences of not taking it. In both instances we will see how much we benefited from those sincere efforts to explore the ramifications of action and inaction.

The first example involves the efforts made by the United States government in 1944–1945 to educate American public opinion about the importance of having a new international body such as the proposed United Nations to replace the defunct League of Nations, and to give it the authority to use collective force if necessary to preserve peace in the world and to prevent a second world war.

In the lead-up to the 1945 international conference in San Francisco in which the United Nations would be born, the U.S. government realized that, before it could sign on to a treaty of such great significance, it would need to have the backing of American public opinion. It needed to convince Americans of the impracticability and dangers of isolationism in a shrinking world. Moreover, it needed to convince them of the necessity of granting an international body, such as the U.N., both the authority and the means to maintain or restore peace and ensure collective security through an international standing force to which members of the United Nations would contribute troops and military equipment.

To obtain public support, the State Department spearheaded a concerted, broad, and systematic campaign to educate the American public. It drew on a wide range of resources to achieve its purpose, including disseminating information by educating top academic practitioners, printing magazine and newspaper articles, publishing books, broadcasting radio programs, and even convincing Hollywood to produce a documentary film about the merits of a United Nations. After intense and focused activity over a period of six months, the State Department had accomplished a widespread educational program. It had distributed around two million copies of a pamphlet about the Dumbarton Oaks proposals for a United Nations to various civic groups; delivered more than 500 speeches to a variety of audiences in all major cities, including people in business, labor, professional leaders and churches; organized an informal exchange of views between the Secretary of State and leading writers and editors; given comprehensive briefings for the benefit of the nation's top international affairs academics; and arranged for a series of instructive radio lectures over the NBC radio network in addition to its successful bid to get Hollywood movie makers to produce a documentary film extolling the virtues of the U.N.[140]

The State Department's efforts were so successful that, after a mere six months, 60 percent of the population of the United States had heard or read about the proposed U.N. Additionally, of those polled, an incredible 81 percent supported both the U.N. and the collective use of force.[141]

The second example of a successful effort to educate public opinion about the benefits of taking a particular course of action is the Federalist Papers. They were a series of eight-five essays written by Alexander Hamilton, James Madison, and John Jay to rebut the arguments of critics of the new constitution proposed in Philadelphia, and thereby convince the people of New York (and other states) that they should ratify the proposed Constitution for a federated United States. Thus, in a historic move, they paved the way for America to move from a confederation to a federation.[142]

By contrast, it is worth exploring a couple of instances of what happens when leaders fail to adequately educate the public about the ramifications of alternative decisions they might make or actions they might pursue. The first example that leaps to mind is climate change. The scientific community has been warning us for years about the escalating dangers of allowing global warming to proceed unchecked. Despite such warnings, leaders around the world have abjectly failed in their responsibility to their populations. They have not taken the time or trouble to patiently and painstakingly present to people the facts, the dangers of inaction, and the benefits of a course correction. Perhaps they have incorrectly assumed that we, the people of the world, would not understand and would not be willing to make the sacrifices necessary to arrest global warming. Yet, they underestimated us. Surely, had we understood what our inaction would mean to our very survival and the quality of life that our children and grandchildren will have to endure we would have been willing to follow their leadership and done what was right and sensible. Or perhaps, they worried that, having been bearers of bad news, they would be booted out of office. Again, they disregarded their role as public servants to act in our best interests and not to do whatever they could to hang on to power, influence, and resources.

A second example is the painful experience of Brexit. At the time when the referendum was first announced, both sides for and against leaving the E.U. engaged in campaigns of misinformation designed to help them win votes. The lies and exaggerations that both sides engaged in obfuscated the truth and truly disserved the British public, the European public, and the world at large, as the ramifications of Brexit affect the entire global community. By the time the British public found out that they had been misled, it was too late—the vote had already been taken and Britain was set on a course of polarization, fueled by high emotions on all sides, entrenchment of positions, and ultimately disunity. Who knows what the result might have been had the people of Britain been told the unvarnished truth about the various short- and long-term consequences of the different choices before them. We shall never know. However, chances are that regardless of whether the British people would have chosen Brexit under such circumstances, their relations with each other would not have been so acrimonious and polarized.

While Brexit certainly has its downsides, it has also created opportunities for potential growth. One of these opportunities is reflected in the fact that people are questioning whether there is a better way to express the will of the people rather than through the imperfect instrument of a referendum that poses very stark questions without allowing for any nuanced reasoning. It has led to some creative ideas, including one proposed by British Parliamentarian

Rory Stewart. He suggested that Britain could try to bridge the gap between a direct democracy represented by a referendum and indirect democracy reflected in parliamentary decisions by creating a citizens' assembly that would represent citizens across the country. It would sit for a short period, limited to three to four few weeks, attempt to ascertain the true will of the people with respect to the question at hand, for instance, Brexit, and then return to Parliament with a fresh mandate from the people.[143] This type of creativity and innovative thinking in order to build unity must be encouraged.

We can gain further understanding of the benefits that accrue when our leaders take the time and care necessary to openly and truthfully share with us the facts involving key decisions by looking at what is currently happening with the coronavirus pandemic. Different governments have taken different approaches in dealing with the crisis. Some have been very transparent about sharing facts with their citizens, no matter how unpleasant the situation is.

From the start of the pandemic, German Chancellor Angela Merkel began informing the German population that experts had informed her government that by the time the pandemic was over, chances were that up to 70 percent of the German population would be infected. She conveyed her message in measured terms and without histrionics. Her openness and style of communication won her the trust of the German people, who were willing to follow their government's guidance in dealing with the pandemic. As a result they soon found themselves in the enviable position of re-opening their economy slowly and methodically in an attempt to avoid a second wave of infections. Although Germany is still not out of the woods yet as of the time of writing this book, it is a lot better off than countries like the United States that never managed to flatten the curve of infections caused by the first wave of the coronavirus and emerge for breath before being subjected to a second wave.

Apart from Germany, a few other countries have been similarly open with their people, including New Zealand and Taiwan. It is noteworthy that the leaders of all these countries are women who have demonstrated a common set of qualities that have served their people well in facing the crisis of the pandemic. These include the willingness to listen, compassion, courage, transparency, honesty, humility, forethought, and flexibility.

By contrast, the leaders of many countries have failed to be open and truthful with their citizens about the dangers of the virus and the strict measures that are required to contain it. Consequently, they have delayed issuing and imposing social distancing guidelines and urging their people to wear masks and wash hands. These delays have been costly in terms of lives lost, human and mental suffering, and economic disruption caused by the consequent need for extended lockdowns. The United States and Brazil are good examples of nations that fall into this second category. Another consequence of this failure by leaders to openly and transparently share information with the public is that the vacuum left has allowed room for misinformation to take root, including about vaccines critical to protecting us all. The absence of leadership in sending a strong clear, consistent message about the efficacy of vaccines has allowed all sorts of conspiracy theories about them to take hold in the minds of the population.

Our exploration of the different scenarios underscores the critical importance of ensuring that we elect leaders who are inclined to openly share with us, their citizens, the dangers and opportunities that face us and who have the habit of providing us with the unvarnished facts. In doing so, they seek to cultivate a unified public opinion based on open consultation and true understanding of the consequences of action or inaction. As nations around the world learn to create relationships between leaders and the governed that are based on openness and mutual respect, we will find that we will move to a unity of thought in how best to tackle global challenges such as climate change.

If we are to succeed in building a peaceful world, our leaders must begin raising awareness among their citizenry not just about the dangers and opportunities that are before us. They must also raise consciousness about the need for us to identify and adopt a shared system of global ethics, including an understanding of why in our interconnected world any one nation can only assure its benefit if it works tirelessly to assure the benefit of the global community. Furthermore, they must create an understanding that each nation must be willing to cede a modicum of its national sovereignty in certain narrow spheres that affect the collective interests of humanity in order to build a new system of global governance fit to respond to the unique needs and challenges of humanity at this stage of its collective growth—the stage of its evolving maturity.

CHOOSING A NEW HABIT: ELECTING LEADERS ON THE BASIS OF QUALITIES, MOTIVES, AND RECORD OF SERVICE

We have determined at great length that our world is faced with multiple global challenges, some of which are existential—like climate change and the COVID-19 pandemic. We have also determined that in order to meet the collective challenges of our time we need to abandon our outworn habits of nationalism and expediency and build a new system of global governance based on a firm foundation of a shared system of global ethics. However, no matter how radically we reform our current institutions or how perfectly we design new global institutions, such steps alone will not assure the well-being, peace, and security of humanity. These institutions will still be susceptible to abuse and corruption if we do not ensure that the people who serve as members of those institutions possess integrity and a sterling character.[144]

If we aspire to regain trust in our elected officials, leaders, and institutions we need to start electing leaders who are fit to serve our collective needs and who are prepared to meet the challenges of our time. Moreover, we need to elect world leaders who can come together, put aside their differences and their self-interest, and work toward the singular objective of creating peace in the world. To this end, we must begin by achieving clarity about the role and duty of a worthy and deserving statesman.

Our first step should be to change our mindset and adjust our perspective on the role of leadership to understand that leadership is really about service to the electorate. Leadership means the willingness to don the robe of duty

171

and responsibility rather than the robe of ego and self-interest. Moreover, the main determinant of whether someone will make a good leader is not their personality, their charisma, or their influence, rather it is whether they are suited to fulfill a particular function for their community. An effective and deserving leader is the individual who sees their main task as working tirelessly and with determination to create the conditions that will ensure the welfare, peace, security, and protection of their people, so that they can actualize their individual and collective potential. We should pay close attention to a candidate's actual capacity and their demonstrated record of service as opposed to their social standing.

In order to properly assess a candidate's suitability to be a true leader as described above, we must actively seek to ascertain that three criteria are met. First, they must possess the following qualities that our discussion above has demonstrated are essential to enlightened leadership. They include: freedom from corruption, which in turn requires that they be high-minded, have purity of intention, and be content with a modest stipend. They must also be free from prejudice and, far from stoking divisions and appealing to our worst instincts, they must actively seek to unify their communities through their words and actions. They must have demonstrated a record of dealing honestly and uprightly in all matters including family life and business dealings. They must be selfless in their efforts and be willing to sacrifice their own interests, including material advantages, for the interests of the community. They must also be willing to disregard their own preferences and inclinations, their likes and dislikes, and focus their minds on what will result in the welfare and happiness of their people and benefit the common interest. They must be willing to serve with singular devotion and determination. They must exhibit a willingness and capacity to listen to different view points in a spirit of humility and with the sole goal of finding the truth that benefits their people. They must evince the qualities of compassion and empathy. They must be resilient and secure in their reliance on a strong moral compass rather than swaying with every shift in the ever-changing criteria of approval and expectation. They must possess a high level of administrative skill and be familiar with all the tools of statecraft, including an understanding of the principles of international relations, and knowledge of domestic and foreign affairs. They must possess undaunted courage to do the right thing, to be transparent and honest with their people, and to take actions that are in the best interests of their people, even if they are not popular.[145]

There are some glimmerings that even among politicians there is a dawning awareness that the public actually values hearing the truth from them, no matter how unpleasant reality may be. An instance of this recognition occurred in an interview given by Rory Stewart on *The Economist's* radio podcast. Mr. Stewart observed that people he had met across the country actually liked being told the truth no matter how unpleasant it seemed, and he encouraged politicians to be more truthful and transparent with the people they served.[146]

Indeed, fitness for leadership does not lie in the ideological platforms a candidate proposes or the promises they make. How often has the electorate of a country put their hopes in such promises that are later broken or remain unfulfilled either because their leaders never intended to follow through on their promises, or circumstances intervened to change their minds, or they were blocked from delivering their promises? Similarly, how often has a politician run on a specific platform, and once in power insisted on implementing those policies despite a change in circumstances that rendered the previous promises detrimental to the common weal? The messy process of Brexit serves as a good example of what happens when our leaders feel bound to follow through on previous promises even though facts emerge that make it clear that the original promise is no longer in the best interests of their people. The question that is worth asking is whether the polarization and disunity that the insistence on delivering on the promise of Brexit brought was worth it and served the population? Time will undoubtedly tell.

What alternative can we pursue? In place of platforms and promises, which often feels like putting the cart before the horse, we should focus first on finding leaders with the right character and trusting them to bring to bear their good will, their skills, and their conscience to make decisions that best serve their people in light of changing circumstances. We need to give them the freedom to be agile and adapt to new realities as they emerge rather than being bound to promises that may have originally seemed beneficial, but that, in the light of new circumstances, may not serve our best interests. In short, we need to begin by electing leaders with the right qualities of character and then trusting them to do the right thing.

This is especially important in a world in which we simply cannot predict what events will occur. Take for example, Britain's experience in electing Boris Johnson as Prime Minister. Both the British electorate and Mr. Johnson fully expected that his main task would be to safely guide Britain into a post-Brexit future. No one could have expected that he would, instead, be dealing with an unprecedented public health crisis coupled with an economic crisis. As though this were not enough he was also confronted with the need to craft an appropriate response to the turmoil occuring in America in reaction to the scourge of structural racism in the aftermath of George Floyd's brutal murder while simultaneously being forced to confront Britain's own racist past.[147]

*The Economis*t reminds us of former U.K. Prime Minister Harold McMillan's response when asked what was likely to throw a government off course: "events, dear boy, events." It goes on to suggest that in light of the reality that we cannot predict what events will occur, the best we can do is to look for certain qualities like basic competence including an ability to think long-term, to pay attention to details, and be consistent.[148]

We have an example of someone who is generally viewed as having been a great statesman—Abraham Lincoln—who followed this approach. He is famously attributed the quote, "I never had a policy; I have just tried to do my very best each and every day," demonstrating a much needed flexibility toward addressing shifting political questions. Rather than acting on the basis of pre-set policies and expectations, Lincoln was able to steer the young union by following his moral compass, even as it developed over time. If we were to elect leaders on this basis, we should then heed our chosen statesmen as best we can, deriving the added benefit of maintaining our national unity by supporting whatever leaders we elected for the duration of their term. Change would come at the ballot box rather than from attempts to undermine an undesirable leader through rancorous, polarizing, and divisive debates. Ultimately, we always have the choice to make change. If we find that they are not performing in our best interests, we can always choose different leaders at the next election.

The second criterion is that leaders should be motivated solely by what promotes the interests of their people, and beyond that, the human race as a whole. They must recognize that, in today's interconnected world, glory comes not from loving one's own country but rather from loving humankind. They must understand that in a world that has effectively become like a single organism, they must tirelessly work to seek the fusion of the interests of all nations rather than to maintain an equilibrium of those interests, a principle that Jean Monnet, father of the European Union, understood viscerally and articulated repeatedly as he laid the foundations for what we know today as the E.U. Their dominant passion in today's world must be to do whatever is necessary to establish international peace and security. They must be willing to consult and collaborate and do whatever is necessary to make this peace a reality, for without it we will continue to needlessly suffer and fail to actualize our collective potential.

The third criterion is that they must have demonstrated that they possess the qualities, capacities, and motivations delineated above through their demonstrated achievements and record of service. Our elected leaders should have a history of service, selflessness, and unity-building in both their professional and personal lives. Their records should demonstrate a consistent willingness to sacrifice their time, energy, and material well-being in order to work for the well-being of their communities. Such service should be rendered solely for the sake of their fellow countrymen rather than out of any desire for power, influence, and self-promotion. Moreover, their records should not be tarnished by injustice, prejudice, corruption, or violence. They should be builders of unity rather than sowers of division and hatred. In short, the proven record of service of candidates for election will demonstrate the quality of character and leadership they will bring to their position as elected officials.

Independent Investigation of Truth

One of the disempowering habits we have as communities is our failure to investigate the truth for ourselves. Instead we tend to abdicate our responsibility by swallowing wholesale any information that is fed to us regardless of the reliability of the source. It is this failure that causes us to elect unfit leaders. It also causes us to make decisions about our collective destiny without the benefit of adequate facts and transparent information, which often results in outcomes that do not serve us.

Our experience in the United States over the past few years has demonstrated the truth of the old statement that some attribute to Mark Twain and others to Jonathan Swift: "A lie can travel halfway around the world while the truth is still putting on its shoes." An example of this disinformation is the increasing phenomenon of "fake news" in recent years. When we are not primed to independently investigate truth we become susceptible to accepting fake news and we are vulnerable to the interested parties that seek to sow disunity and division among us. Even without the scourge of fake news, we have a tendency to limit our spheres of information and influence to small echo chambers that continuously perpetuate the same set of ideas and perspectives within a small community. This tendency limits our understanding of reality, which in turn limits the range of choices we perceive as being available to us, and ultimately leads to similar results that do not improve our situation. We can best understand this limitation by thinking of truth as a multi-faceted gem. Depending on the vantage point from which we view it and the angle at which the light happens to hit the gem, we may observe different colors. A person situated one particular way may see the gem as red, while another person looking from a different vantage point may see it as yellow or blue. If each group is tenaciously attached to their fixed viewpoint then their understanding of the facets of the gem are severely limited. It is only by a willingness to look at things from one another's perspectives that our collective understanding is enhanced and the range of possibilities open to us is broadened.

To the extent that we hone the skill of independently investigating the truth we will be less susceptible to being manipulated by interests that seek to serve their own agendas by sowing doubts in our minds, creating suspicions and ultimately confusion that make us turn against each other. Indeed, our well-being and ability to thrive as a nation will depend on the speed with which we develop this habit.

If we are to successfully develop a new habit of electing worthy and deserving leaders, we must first develop and hone our ability to investigate the truth in determining their qualities, motivations, and record of service in a manner that is free of preconceived prejudices. We tend to be particularly susceptible to such prejudices when we are emotionally influenced, either positively or negatively. When we are strongly attached to a person or group of people and feel emotionally connected to them and what they represent to us, we often follow them without critically examining their character and quality of leadership. Similarly, we are inclined to judge harshly when we strongly dislike or even hate an idea, a person or a group of people and feel repelled by them. In order to dispassionately assess the truth we must practice detaching ourselves from our predisposition to strongly like or dislike a person or their views.

Next we must be willing to gauge the truth for ourselves, choosing to see reality and assess it with our own knowledge, using our minds, hearts, and intuition. It is critical that we own this responsibility to ascertain the truth rather than abdicating it to others. As we set about the task of seeking the truth, it is crucial that we focus on empirical information rather than opinion. This requires great vigilance and discipline in sifting fact from opinion. This is a particularly difficult task in today's world in which we are so immersed in a media culture dominated by gossip that seeks to build up and tear down individuals and systems through hearsay and idle chatter.

Another growing phenomenon is to abdicate responsibility for personal investigation by questioning the very existence of truth. In his book, *On Tyranny,* Timothy Snyder, professor of history at Yale University writes about the trend of "generic cynicism" that "makes us feel hip and alternative even as we slip along with our fellow citizens into a morass of indifference." Rather than foraging for truth and discerning fact from fiction, we hide behind the new wave of cynicism and lull ourselves into justified inaction.[149] We must resist this tempting pull toward apathetic resignation and we must quest to find truth, no matter how challenging or painful the process might be.

We must also begin to demand that our media becomes independent of all private and public interests and that its only role is to faithfully report the facts without layering on opinions. We should trust in our judgment to arrive at our own conclusions. As we approach our collective stage of maturity, we should be accorded the respect of being allowed to understand the truth for ourselves without the intermediary of either clergy or talking heads who drown us in their opinions as though they were the truth.

In our efforts to ascertain the truth we must be wary of the pitfall of believing that the truth lies in the middle of opposing views and requires a compromise between different perspectives. We have already seen the damage that such an approach has caused in the area of climate change. One of the reasons why it was so difficult to convey the empirical facts about the reality of climate change, as well as the enormous threats it poses to the public, is because the media would organize panel discussions in which the two opposing views about climate change would be discussed. Even though roughly 97 percent of active climate scientists agreed that climate change was real, that it was caused by human activity, and that it posed an imminent threat to humanity, the time devoted to discussion on these panels was allocated on an equal basis so that the climate change deniers who represented the views of a miniscule, almost insignificant fraction of climate change scientists was given a disproportionate say. By allocating half of the time to them to advance their position, the media made it appear that it was a toss-up as to whether climate change was real or not.

As we seek to identify people fit to serve us as leaders, it is important that we expand our notion of whose interests we are considering. Far from considering whether a person's views will benefit us as individuals, we must train ourselves to think in terms of the interests of a global society. We must transcend thinking in terms of individual, local, and even national interests, and remind ourselves that in today's interconnected world in which humanity has become a single organism, the benefit of our communities—local or national—can only be ensured by guaranteeing the benefit of all of humanity.

Turning a Blind Eye to Injustice

This book would not be complete without mentioning a collective habit that is so poisonous that it corrodes the very fabric of our society, and affects every level of proposed change in this work—namely the habit of allowing injustice and discrimination in all its various hues to fester and destroy the very essence of what defines us as human, and to corrode the foundations of all our societal systems, be they economic, social, political, or religious. Our elected leaders and institutions have historically turned a blind eye to injustices within their own spheres of influence, as well as in the international community, preferring to protect their economic and political self-interest over the lives and freedom of other human beings.

Injustice is a multi-headed hydra. It manifests in the horrors of racism, such as the pervasive, continuing violence against and oppression of Black Americans in the United States. It appears in ethnic and religious prejudice as reflected in the persecution of the Uighur community in China, the Rohingya community in Myanmar, and many more persecuted groups around the world. It is reflected in the excessive and growing disparities between the rich

181

and the poor. It manifests itself in all forms of discrimination based on gender, including the repression and abuse of women. We see it in the horrific statistics of domestic violence in so many countries around the world. Unfortunately, injustice surrounds us, and examples of it and the destructive effects it brings abound.

Manifestations of injustice lie at the crossroads between prejudice and self-interest. Currently, many of our systems and cultures of power and domination allow for these two to fester and feed into one another. However, prejudice is based on a fundamental misunderstanding of our nature as human beings. It fails to recognize our inextricable interconnectedness and oneness, and it seeks to put inordinate emphasis on the external, superficial aspects of who we are over the reality of our nature as human beings who are expressions of a universal consciousness marked by love, who are striving to live lives of meaning, purpose, and contribution as we actualize our individual potential, and who are each endeavoring to gain those qualities that make us forces for good in this world of darkness.

Striving for Justice at Every Turn

"The purpose of justice is the appearance of unity among men."[150]

"The well-being of mankind, its peace and security, are unattainable unless and until its unity is firmly established."[151]

Justice is the only sure foundation upon which we can build unity and a lasting peace—a world in which the conditions are present for each individual, each component group of people, each nation, and international society as a whole to fulfill its individual and collective potential. Justice is an indispensable guide in consultation, a tool for the collective investigation of reality. It enables us to distinguish truth from falsehood, and is therefore a powerful tool in addressing social inequities. It is the bedrock of order and tranquility in the world. Incorporating justice into the very DNA of the new world we are building—for instance, electing and supporting leaders whose primary aim is striving for justice at every turn—enables us to create unity of thought as well as unity of action. It is only once unity, born of justice, is firmly in place that we can build a lasting peace.

Ultimately, justice is a product of a deep understanding of the oneness, the interconnectedness, and the interdependence of humanity, a theme that has been a pivotal element of this book. It is a prerequisite for every shift in mindset and habit offered in this book. Without it, none of the changes proposed here will endure. Put another way, "justice is the practical expression of awareness that, in the achievement of human progress, the interests of the individual and those of society are inextricably linked."[152]

Conclusion:
Choosing New
Mindsets and Habits
Will Lead Us to a Lasting Peace

This book maps out a viable route we can collectively take to reach our goal of a peaceful and secure world. To fulfill our desire for peace we must first be willing to honestly assess where we are, and accept full responsibility for our past choices of mindsets and behaviors that have led us to this current moment. The next step is to create a vision of the sort of world we actually want to have—a world marked by peace and security. More specifically, we need to have a compelling vision of what the relationships between three protagonists of a global society, namely the individual, the community, and governing institutions look like. When these relationships are harmonious, mutually reinforcing, and supportive, they will generate the conditions to support us in fulfilling our individual and collective potential. Once we have identified that vision it is critical that we cultivate a feeling of faith and absolute certainty that we can achieve that vision, and commit wholeheartedly and without hesitation to achieving it. Having committed ourselves to making our vision a reality we must work tirelessly and with ceaseless effort to close the gap between where we are and we want to be. We will only do so by mindfully and consistently adopting the new mindsets and habits proposed in this book to get us to our goal.

The process outlined here can be captured by reflecting on the following metaphor. Imagine that we are on land and we want to set sail for a destination that we believe exists but that we have never before seen. As we look out over the horizon all we see is a small island in the distance but there is no evidence of the final destination. At this point our only hope of success is to believe that we will reach our destination, and commit to setting sail in the direction of the island. It is only as we make the choice to move and make progress toward this first milestone that our horizon moves to encompass more opportunities, new vistas open up, and we start to see other islands further away. With each leg of this journey and with sustained effort and determination we will get closer to our destination, until one day it is in full view and visibly within reach.

Humanity stands at a critical crossroads. We have arrived at a critical moment of choice. We can exercise our gift of free will to continue on our current path, stubbornly clinging to our long-entrenched dysfunctional collective mindsets that have spawned destructive collective habits. Alternatively, we can choose the proverbial third path discussed earlier, leading to a better future for ourselves and grounded in a firm understanding that our fates and fortunes rise and fall together. Choosing this path will guide us to a future in which our world is finally at peace, secure, and fit to create an environment in which we can grow on all fronts: spiritually, intellectually, emotionally, and materially. In this new environment, our growth in all spheres can be balanced, allowing us to actualize the full range of our potential.

Should we choose to take up the challenge offered in this book and adopt the new perspectives and habits it proposes, we will create the unity of thought and action necessary to propel us forward to a brighter future and finally put an end to our endless mental suffering, to conflict, war and self-destruction on an unprecedented scale. We will save ourselves from the severe lag in collective growth that has resulted from humanity becoming stuck in the adolescent stage of its development. Instead of indulging in feelings of helplessness and anger that cause apathy, conflict, and blame, we will begin to take responsibility for our collective plight and take steps to create a new way of being and a new global order, thereby putting an end to unnecessary suffering. We will truly have understood our oneness as people and nations, choosing to learn from our past suffering and turn it into opportunities to begin a new way of being.

Accordingly, we will move to the next phase in our collective growth marked by the creation of a political peace, namely a cessation of war. We will also create a new system of global governance fit to meet our needs at this stage of maturity. A majority of states will initially commit themselves to this system, which will comprise collective decision-making institutions capable of passing international laws binding on all nations, and a system of collective security that ensures that the collectively agreed-upon laws are enforced. This new system of global governance will be grounded in collective consultation, collaboration, and cooperation. This next phase in our collective development will afford us the means to tackle some key global challenges, including the ones that pose threats to our very survival such as nuclear proliferation, pandemics, and climate change. In this next phase of our growth we will arrest the cycle of destruction and achieve a modicum of stability. At this point we may find that this stage in our collective evolution has its limits and that we need to reach for a deeper unity that goes beyond a political peace and takes into account our spiritual reality in order to resolve at root, once and for all, some of our deeper social problems like religious animosity and racism. Tackling these deeper challenges will require us to move to a new level of growth and collective healing, which is the subject for another book.

For now, let us resolve that we will rise to the challenge set before us. Let us both individually and collectively deliberate and choose to don a new set of lenses through which to perceive and understand our social reality. With this fresh basis for understanding and a new set of empowering habits, let us lay a sure foundation for a durable peace. We must work tirelessly and not rest until we have achieved this worthy goal.

Acknowledgments

There are several people to whom I owe a substantial debt of gratitude. First is my daughter, Gigi Ewing, who graciously undertook the painstaking task of editing this book multiple times over the course of months. The many hours we spent together during the Covid-19 pandemic, poring over the structure of the book, the flow, and the details, while sometimes emotionally trying, yielded many rewards, the greatest of which was working on a joint mother-daughter endeavor aimed at contributing toward world peace.

An equally great debt of gratitude goes to my husband, Ken Ewing, who once again spent countless hours formatting and designing the book's layout, ensuring that the citations and bibliography were correct, and attending to the myriad thankless details that immeasurably enhanced the quality of the book. Best of all, he did this without complaint.

I am also deeply grateful beyond measure to a handful of friends who cheered me along especially in those moments when my energy was flagging. They include Enid Valentine, Cindy Wallace, Vasu Mohan, Aditya Guthey, and Maggie Paxson.

Notes

1. Bahá'u'lláh and Shoghi Effendi, *Gleanings*.
2. Churchill, *Liberalism and the Social Problem*.
3. Economist Staff, "The Coronavirus Spreads Racism Against—and Among—Ethnic Chinese," February 17, 2020.
4. NAACP, "Criminal Justice Fact Sheet".
5. Godoy and Wood, "What Do Coronavirus Racial Disparities Look Like State by State?"; Centers for Disease Control and Prevention National Center for Health Statistics, "Health Equity Considerations and Racial and Ethnic Minority Groups," July 24, 2020; AP Staff, "People of Color, Women Shoulder Front-Line Work During Pandemic," May 4, 2020.
6. Kingkade, "Rise in Domestic Violence"; *Stopping Lockdown Domestic Abuse on My Street*.
7. Intergovernmental Science-Policy Platform on Biodiversity and Ecosystem Services, "Media Release".
8. Turkewitz, "The Amazon Is on Fire. So Is Central Africa."; Kann, "The Amazon Is a Key Buffer Against Climate Change. A New Study Warns Wildfires Could Decimate It".
9. Pierre-Louis, "The Amazon, Siberia, Indonesia".
10. Calma, "What You Need to Know about the Australia Bushfires".
11. Mecklin, "Current Time".
12. Baum, "The Risk of Nuclear Winter".
13. Universal House of Justice, "Message on World Peace," January 18, 2019.

14. Centers for Disease Control and Prevention National Center for Health Statistics, "CDC Mental Health Survey," October 2020.
15. Pew Research Center, "Public's Mood Turns Grim; Trump Trails Biden on Most Personal Traits, Major Issues".
16. Loria, "The World Health Organisation Is Worried about Disease x and You Should Be Too".
17. Daszak, "We Knew Disease x Was Coming. It's Here Now."; Sanger et al., "Before Virus Outbreak, a Cascade of Warnings Went Unheeded"; Schmidt, "Coronavirus Researchers Tried to Warn Us"; SciTechDaily Staff, "Scientists Warned China Was a 'Time Bomb' for Novel Coronavirus Outbreak in 2007".
18. Economist Staff, "Global Leadership Is Missing in Action," June 18, 2020.
19. Jabr, "How Does a Caterpillar Turn into a Butterfly?".
20. Kissinger, "The Coronavirus Pandemic Will Forever Alter the World Order".
21. United Nations, "The Recovery from the COVID-19 Crisis Must Lead to a Different Economy".
22. Ma'ani-Ewing, "Peace and Collective Security," March 7, 2020.
23. Hatcher, "The Concept of Spirituality".
24. Camus and O'Brien, *The Myth of Sisyphus and Other Essays*.
25. Kupferschmidt, "'A Completely New Culture of Doing Research.' Coronavirus Outbreak Changes How Scientists Communicate".
26. Achor, *The Happiness Advantage*, 2010, 109.
27. Achor, 108.
28. France 24 Staff, "French Politicians Accuse US of Buying up Chinese Face Masks Bound for France".

29. Smith, "New York's Andrew Cuomo Decries 'eBay'-Style Bidding War for Ventilators".
30. Dyer, *When You Change the Way You Look at Things.*
31. Shoghi Effendi, *Call to the Nations.*
32. Toynbee, *Change and Habit*, 138–39.
33. Henley, *Book of Verses.*, 57.
34. Frankl, *Man's Search for Meaning*, 65–67.
35. Frankl, 133–34.
36. Achor, *The Happiness Advantage*, 2010, 108–9.
37. Ministry for Europe {and} Foreign Affairs, "A Strong Europe in a World of Uncertainties"; Bahá'u'lláh and Shoghi Effendi, *Gleanings.*
38. Horsey, "Nelson Mandela Transformed Himself and Then His Nation".
39. Ashe, "Nelson Mandela the Love and Forgiveness Project".
40. Hibbs, "Mandela".
41. Glanz and Robertson, "Lockdown Delays Cost at Least 36,000 Lives, Data Show".
42. Scripps Research Institute, "Up to 45 Percent of SARS-CoV-2 Infections May Be Asymptomatic".
43. Godman, "Have One Autoimmune Disease? You May Be at Risk for Another".
44. CNN Editorial Research, "Syrian Civil War Fast Facts," April 9, 2020.
45. Peçanha, Almukhtar, and Lai, "Untangling the Overlapping Conflicts in the Syrian War".
46. Lee, *America for Americans*, 148.
47. Washington Post Staff, "Full Text".
48. Santora, "Poland Bashes Immigrants, but Quietly Takes Christian Ones (Published 2019)".
49. Horowitz, "Italy's Right Links Low Birthrate to Fight Against Abortion and Migration (Published 2019)".

50. Washington, "Farewell Address - Saturday, September 17, 1796".
51. Donadio, "France's Yellow Vests Are Rebels Without a Cause".
52. Singh, "Nationalism Can Have Its Good Points. Really.".
53. Staff, "The Mighty Nile, Threatened by Waste, Warming, Mega-Dam".
54. Telegraph Foreign Staff, "Death of the Nile".
55. AP Staff, "US Suspends Millions in Aid to Ethiopia over Nile Dam Dispute," September 3, 2020.
56. Economist Staff, "How to Save the Euro," September 17, 2011.
57. Cooper and Lowrey, "Eyeing 2012, White House Presses Europe on Debt".
58. IAEA, "Additional Protocol".
59. Sanger and Jakes, "Iran Is Accused of Hiding Suspected Nuclear Activity".
60. Mazzetti, Sanger, and Broad, "U.s. Examines Whether Saudi Nuclear Program Could Lead to Bomb Effort".
61. BBC Staff, "Climate Change," December 10, 2019.
62. Larson and Brown, "Scientists Seek Rare Species Survivors Amid Australia Flames".
63. Welz, "Fire Fallout".
64. Brown and Larson, "Fires Set Stage for Irreversible Forest Losses in Australia".
65. NYT Staff, "Suspect Is Charged with Arson in Oregon Wildfire".
66. Rio, "Dry Thunderstorms Could Accelerate the California Wildfires".
67. Symonds, "Amazon Rainforest Fires".
68. Turkewitz, "The Amazon Is on Fire. So Is Central Africa.".

69. Economist Staff, "Siberia's Heatwave Would Not Have Happened Without Climate Change," July 15, 2020.
70. Khurshudyan, "Wildfires Ravaged Siberia Last Year. This Spring, the Blazes Are Starting Even Bigger.".
71. Intergovernmental Panel on Climate Change, "Summary for Policymakers of IPCC Special Report on Global Warming of 1.5°c Approved by Governments".
72. Titley, "Why Is Climate Change's 2 Degrees Celsius of Warming Limit so Important?".
73. Gustin, "The Paris Climate Problem".
74. Ripple et al., "World Scientists' Warning of a Climate Emergency".
75. United Nations FCCC Conference of the Parties, "Paris Agreement".
76. Reuters Staff, "Timeline," January 15, 2020.
77. Norland, "Trade War Costs to Consumers, Companies and Nations".
78. DeBarros, "Trade War with China Took Toll on u.s., But Not Big One".
79. Achor, *Before Happiness*, 2013.
80. Ignatius, "Coronavirus Will Test Whether the Planet Can Unite in the Face of a Global Crisis".
81. "Communication, Collaboration and Cooperation Can Stop the 2019 Coronavirus".
82. Apuzzo and Kirkpatrick, "Covid-19 Changed How the World Does Science, Together".
83. 'Abdu'l-Bahá, *Selections from the Writings of 'abdu'l-Bahá*.
84. Goldin, *Divided Nations*.
85. McElvoy, *The Economist Asks*, n.d..
86. Schell, *The Seventh Decade*, 217; Naím, *The End of Power*, 238.

87. Economist Staff, "Countries Look at Ways to Tinker with Earth's Thermostat," March 14, 2019.
88. Laya, "Opinion \Textbar as We Fight the Pandemic, It's Clear the World Wasn't Ready. Here's How to Fix That.".
89. Elliot, "Gordon Brown Calls for Global Government to Tackle Coronavirus".
90. Stockholm International Peace Research Institute, "Global Military Expenditure Sees Largest Annual Increase in a Decade—Says SIPRI—Reaching $1917 Billion in 2019".
91. Larson, "New Research"; Bulgarella, "Why the Increased Diversity of the Next Congress Is a Victory for Ethics"; Kelman et al., "'Tell It Like It Is'".
92. United Nations High Commissioner for Refugees, "Figures at a Glance".
93. Matthew Lee, Gannon, Kathy, and Altman, Howard, "All US Troops to Leave Afghanistan in 14 Months If Taliban Meets Commitments of Peace Deal".
94. Casey and Krauss, "It Doesn't Matter If Ecuador Can Afford This Dam. China Still Gets Paid. (Published 2018)".
95. Rácz, "African Comeback".
96. Myers, "China's Voracious Appetite for Timber Stokes Fury in Russia and Beyond".
97. Taylor, "Personal Growth".
98. Mahbubani, "The Boat Adrift".
99. Universal House of Justice, "October 1985 - to the Peoples of the World," October 1985.
100. Lamy, "Global Governance".
101. Goldin, *Divided Nations*, 167.
102. International Commission on Intervention and State Sovereignty et al., *The Responsibility to Protect*.
103. United Nations, *In Larger Freedom*, 2005.

104. United Nations General Assembly, "Resolution Adopted by the General Assembly on 16 September 2005".
105. Roosevelt and Churchill, "The Atlantic Charter".
106. Erlanger and Stevis-Gridneff, "Angela Merkel Guides the e.u. To a Deal, However Imperfect".
107. Erlanger, "One Crisis Too Many".
108. Stevis-Gridneff, "A €750 Billion Virus Recovery Plan Thrusts Europe into a New Frontier".
109. Ma'ani-Ewing, *Bridge to Global Governance*, 2018.
110. The International Crisis Group, "The Responsibility to Protect".
111. Levi and O'Hanlon, *The Future of Arms Control*.
112. CNN Editorial Research, "Iraq Weapons Inspections Fast Facts," March 16, 2020.
113. Blix, *Disarming Iraq*, 4, 11.
114. BBC Staff, "Beirut Explosion," August 11, 2020.
115. Reuters Staff, "Beirut Port Blast Death Toll Rises to 190," August 30, 2020.
116. Hubbard, "As Smoke Clears in Beirut, Shock Turns to Anger".
117. Guardian Staff, "The Observer View on the Failure to Secure a Global Ceasefire During the Pandemic \Textbar Observer Editorial".
118. Jones, "The Fall of Rajoy".
119. Felter and Labrador, "Brazil's Corruption Fallout".
120. Sang-Hun, "Park Geun-Hye, Ex-South Korean Leader, Gets 25 Years in Prison (Published 2018)".
121. Onishi and Gebrekidan, "South Africa Vows to End Corruption. Are Its New Leaders Part of the Problem?".
122. Willsher, "François Fillon Found Guilty of Embezzling Public Funds".

123. BBC Staff, "Why Is There a War in Syria?" February 25, 2019.
124. Albert and Maizland, "The Rohingya Crisis".
125. Ellis-Petersen, "India Strips Kashmir of Special Status and Divides It in Two".
126. BBC Staff, "Citizenship Amendment Bill," December 11, 2019.
127. Biswas, "Ayodhya Verdict".
128. Gettleman and Kumar, "Modi Founds Temple on Mosque's Ruins, in Triumphal Moment for Hindu Base".
129. Baha'i World News Service, "Iran's Secret Blueprint for the Destruction of the Baha'i Community".
130. Baha'i International Community Representative Offices, "Situation of Baha'is in Iran".
131. CNN Staff, "Iran 'Plans to Destroy Baha'i Community' - CNN.com".
132. Urban Institute, "Structural Racism in America".
133. WION Web Team, "Curfew Imposed in 40 Cities Including Washington DC as Protests Spread Across US".
134. Gibbs, "When a President Can't Be Taken at His Word".
135. Rich, "Losing Earth".
136. Economist Staff, "The Quest for Prosperity," March 17, 2007.
137. United Nations News Staff, "Greta Thunberg Tells World Leaders 'You Are Failing Us,' as Nations Announce Fresh Climate Action".
138. Economist Staff, "As Inequality Grows, so Does the Political Influence of the Rich," July 21, 2018.
139. Rohn and Widener, *Twelve Pillars*.
140. Hoopes and Brinkley, *FDR and the Creation of the u.n.*.
141. Hoopes and Brinkley.
142. Hamilton et al., *The Federalist Papers*.

143. Chotiner, "Rory Stewart Insists That Brexit Is Different from Trump".
144. 'Abdu'l-Bahá, Gail, and Khan, *The Secret of Divine Civilization*, 16–18.
145. 'Abdu'l-Bahá, Gail, and Khan, *The Secret of Divine Civilization*.
146. McElvoy, *Who Can Lead Britain Through Brexit?*.
147. Landler and Castle, "As Prime Minister, Boris Johnson Struggles to Find His Voice".
148. Economist Staff, "Britain Has the Wrong Government for the Covid Crisis," June 18, 2020; Economist Staff, "The British State Shows How Not to Respond to a Pandemic," June 20, 2020.
149. Snyder, *On Tyranny*, 73.
150. Bahá'u'lláh, *Tablets of Bahá'u'lláh, Revealed After the Kitáb-i-Aqdas*, 67.
151. Bahá'u'lláh and Shoghi Effendi, *Gleanings*.
152. Bahá'í International Community, *The Prosperity of Humankind*.

Bibliography

Achor, Shawn. *Before Happiness: The 5 Hidden Keys to Achieving Success, Spreading Happiness, and Sustaining Positive Change*. New York: Crown Business, 2013.

———. *The Happiness Advantage: The Seven Principles of Positive Psychology That Fuel Success and Performance at Work*. 1st ed. New York: Broadway Books, 2010.

Albert, Eleanor, and Lindsay Maizland. "The Rohingya Crisis. The Council on Foreign Relations," January 23, 2020. https://www.cfr.org/backgrounder/rohingya-crisis.

AP Staff. "People of Color, Women Shoulder Front-Line Work During Pandemic. NBC News," May 4, 2020. https://www.nbcnews.com/news/nbcblk/people-color-women-shoulder-front-line-work-during-pandemic-n1199291.

———. "US Suspends Millions in Aid to Ethiopia over Nile Dam Dispute. France 24," September 3, 2020. https://www.france24.com/en/20200902-us-suspends-millions-in-aid-to-ethiopia-over-nile-dam-dispute.

Apuzzo, Matt, and David D. Kirkpatrick. "Covid-19 Changed How the World Does Science, Together." *The New York Times*, April 2, 2020, 1. https://www.nytimes.com/2020/04/01/world/europe/coronavirus-science-research-cooperation.html.

Ashe, Thomas. "Nelson Mandela the Love and Forgiveness Project. Love & Forgiveness in Governance." Accessed October 11, 2020. https://blogs.shu.edu/diplomacyresearch/2013/12/11/an-exemplar-of-forgiving-prisoner-nelson-mandela/.

Baha'i International Community Representative Offices.

"Situation of Baha'is in Iran: Current Situation. Focus Areas," August 2020. https://www.bic.org/focus-areas/situation-iranian-bahais/current-situation.

Baha'i World News Service. "Iran's Secret Blueprint for the Destruction of the Baha'i Community." Accessed October 12, 2020. https://news.bahai.org/human-rights/iran/education/feature-articles/secret-blueprint.

Bahá'u'lláh. *Tablets of Bahá'u'lláh, Revealed After the Kitáb-i-Aqdas.* 1st ed. Haifa : Wilmette, Ill: The Centre ; Distributed in the U.S. by Bahá'í Pub. Trust, 1978, n.d.

Bahá'í International Community. *The Prosperity of Humankind: A Statement.* London: Bahá'í Publishing Trust, 1995.

Bahá'u'lláh, and Shoghi Effendi. *Gleanings from the Writings of Bahá'u'lláh.* New ed. Wilmette, Ill: Bahá'í Pub, 2005.

Baum, Seth. "The Risk of Nuclear Winter. Federation of American Scientists," May 29, 2015. https://fas.org/pir-pubs/risk-nuclear-winter/.

BBC Staff. "Beirut Explosion: What We Know so Far. BBC News," August 11, 2020. https://www.bbc.com/news/world-middle-east-53668493.

———. "Citizenship Amendment Bill: India's New 'Anti-Muslim' Law Explained. BBC News," December 11, 2019. https://www.bbc.com/news/world-asia-india-50670393.

———. "Climate Change: Greenland's Ice Is Melting Faster Than Expected. BBC News," December 10, 2019. https://www.bbc.co.uk/newsround/50729990.

———. "Profile: EU's Jean-Claude Juncker. BBC News," July 15, 2014. https://www.bbc.com/news/world-europe-27679170.

———. "Why Is There a War in Syria? BBC News," February

25, 2019. https://www.bbc.com/news/world-middle-east-35806229.

Biswas, Soutik. "Ayodhya Verdict: Indian Top Court Gives Holy Site to Hindus. BBC News," November 9, 2019. https://www.bbc.com/news/world-asia-india-50355775.

Blix, Hans. *Disarming Iraq*. 1st ed. New York: Pantheon Books, 2004.

Brown, Matthew, and Christina Larson. "Fires Set Stage for Irreversible Forest Losses in Australia," January 18, 2020. https://abcnews.go.com/Technology/wireStory/fires-set-stage-irreversible-forest-losses-australia-68380818.

Bulgarella, Caterina. "Why the Increased Diversity of the Next Congress Is a Victory for Ethics. Forbes," November 19, 2018. https://www.forbes.com/sites/caterinabulgarella/2018/11/19/why-the-increased-diversity-of-the-next-congress-is-a-victory-for-ethics/.

Calma, Justine. "What You Need to Know about the Australia Bushfires. The Verge," February 13, 2020. https://www.theverge.com/2020/1/3/21048891/australia-wildfires-koalas-climate-change-bushfires-deaths-animals-damage.

Camus, Albert, and Justin O'Brien. *The Myth of Sisyphus and Other Essays*. 1st Vintage international ed. New York: Vintage Books, 1991.

Casey, Nicholas, and Clifford Krauss. "It Doesn't Matter If Ecuador Can Afford This Dam. China Still Gets Paid. (Published 2018)." *The New York Times*, December 25, 2018, 1. https://www.nytimes.com/2018/12/24/world/americas/ecuador-china-dam.html.

Centers for Disease Control and Prevention National Center for Health Statistics. "Anxiety and Depression: Household Pulse Survey. National Center for Health Statistics,"

October 2020. https://www.cdc.gov/nchs/covid19/pulse/mental-health.htm.

———. "Health Equity Considerations and Racial and Ethnic Minority Groups. Centers for Disease Control and Prevention," July 24, 2020. https://www.cdc.gov/coronavirus/2019-ncov/community/health-equity/race-ethnicity.html.

Chotiner, Isaac. "Rory Stewart Insists That Brexit Is Different from Trump. The New Yorker," June 12, 2019. https://www.newyorker.com/news/q-and-a/rory-stewart-insists-that-brexit-is-different-from-trump.

Churchill, Winston S. *Liberalism and the Social Problem*. Teddington, UK: Echo Library, 2007.

CNN Editorial Research. "Iraq Weapons Inspections Fast Facts. CNN," March 16, 2020. https://www.cnn.com/2013/10/30/world/meast/iraq-weapons-inspections-fast-facts/index.html.

———. "Syrian Civil War Fast Facts. CNN," April 9, 2020. https://www.cnn.com/2013/08/27/world/meast/syria-civil-war-fast-facts/index.html.

CNN Staff. "Iran 'Plans to Destroy Baha'i Community' - CNN.com. CNN," May 22, 2008. https://www.cnn.com/2008/WORLD/meast/05/22/iran.bahais/index.html?iref=nextin.

"Communication, Collaboration and Cooperation Can Stop the 2019 Coronavirus." *Nature Medicine* 26, no. 2 (February 2020): 151–51. https://doi.org/10.1038/s41591-020-0775-x.

Cooper, Helene, and Annie Lowrey. "Eyeing 2012, White House Presses Europe on Debt." *The New York Times*, December 7, 2011, 20. https://www.nytimes.com/2011/12/08/world/europe/eyeing-2012-race-white-house-presses-europe-on-debt.html.

Daszak, Peter. "We Knew Disease x Was Coming. It's Here Now. The New York Times," February 27, 2020. https://www.nytimes.com/2020/02/27/opinion/coronavirus-pandemics.html.

DeBarros, Josh Zumbrun {and} Anthony. "Trade War with China Took Toll on u.s., But Not Big One." *Wall Street Journal*, January 13, 2020. https://www.wsj.com/articles/trade-war-with-china-took-toll-on-u-s-but-not-big-one-11578832381?st=txn2521p75c9c1q.

Donadio, Rachel. "France's Yellow Vests Are Rebels Without a Cause. The Atlantic," March 18, 2019. https://www.theatlantic.com/international/archive/2019/03/france-yellow-vest-protesters-want/585160/.

Dyer, Wayne. *When You Change the Way You Look at Things*. Accessed October 10, 2020. https://www.youtube.com/watch?v=CmCkvamDZLs.

Economist Staff. "As Inequality Grows, so Does the Political Influence of the Rich." *The Economist*, July 21, 2018. https://www.economist.com/finance-and-economics/2018/07/21/as-inequality-grows-so-does-the-political-influence-of-the-rich.

———. "Britain Has the Wrong Government for the Covid Crisis." *The Economist*, June 18, 2020. https://www.economist.com/leaders/2020/06/18/britain-has-the-wrong-government-for-the-covid-crisis.

———. "Countries Look at Ways to Tinker with Earth's Thermostat." *The Economist*, March 14, 2019. https://www.economist.com/science-and-technology/2019/03/14/countries-look-at-ways-to-tinker-with-earths-thermostat.

———. "Global Leadership Is Missing in Action." *The*

Economist, June 18, 2020. https://www.economist.com/special-report/2020/06/18/global-leadership-is-missing-in-action.

———. "How to Save the Euro." *The Economist*, September 17, 2011. https://www.economist.com/leaders/2011/09/17/how-to-save-the-euro.

———. "Siberia's Heatwave Would Not Have Happened Without Climate Change." *The Economist*, July 15, 2020. https://www.economist.com/science-and-technology/2020/07/15/siberias-heatwave-would-not-have-happened-without-climate-change.

———. "The British State Shows How Not to Respond to a Pandemic." *The Economist*, June 20, 2020. https://www.economist.com/britain/2020/06/19/the-british-state-shows-how-not-to-respond-to-a-pandemic.

———. "The Coronavirus Spreads Racism Against—and Among—Ethnic Chinese." *The Economist*, February 17, 2020. https://www.economist.com/china/2020/02/17/the-coronavirus-spreads-racism-against-and-among-ethnic-chinese.

———. "The Quest for Prosperity." *The Economist*, March 17, 2007. https://www.economist.com/special-report/2007/03/17/the-quest-for-prosperity.

Elliot, Larry. "Gordon Brown Calls for Global Government to Tackle Coronavirus. The Guardian," March 26, 2020. https://www.theguardian.com/politics/2020/mar/26/gordon-brown-calls-for-global-government-to-tackle-coronavirus.

Ellis-Petersen, Hannah. "India Strips Kashmir of Special Status and Divides It in Two. The Guardian," October 31, 2019. https://www.theguardian.com/world/2019/oct/31/india-strips-kashmir-of-special-status-and-divides-it-in-two.

Erlanger, Steven. "One Crisis Too Many: How the Coronavirus Pushed Germany to Shift Course." *The New York Times*, May 19, 2020, 6. https://www.nytimes.com/2020/05/19/world/europe/coronavirus-germany-merkel-france.html.

Erlanger, Steven, and Matina Stevis-Gridneff. "Angela Merkel Guides the e.u. To a Deal, However Imperfect. The New York Times," July 21, 2020. https://www.nytimes.com/2020/07/21/world/europe/european-union-coronavirus-aid.html.

Felter, Claire, and Rocio Cara Labrador. "Brazil's Corruption Fallout. Council on Foreign Relations," November 7, 2018. https://www.cfr.org/backgrounder/brazils-corruption-fallout.

France 24 Staff. "French Politicians Accuse US of Buying up Chinese Face Masks Bound for France. France 24," April 3, 2020. https://www.france24.com/en/20200403-french-politicians-accuse-us-of-buying-up-chinese-face-masks-bound-for-france.

Frankl, Viktor Emil. *Man's Search for Meaning*. Mini book ed. Boston: Beacon Press, 2006.

Gettleman, Jeffrey, and Hari Kumar. "Modi Founds Temple on Mosque's Ruins, in Triumphal Moment for Hindu Base." *The New York Times*, August 5, 2020, 9. https://www.nytimes.com/2020/08/05/world/asia/modi-temple-ayodhya.html.

Gibbs, Nancy. "When a President Can't Be Taken at His Word." *Time*, April 3, 2017. https://time.com/4710615/donald-trump-truth-falsehoods/.

Glanz, James, and Campbell Robertson. "Lockdown Delays Cost at Least 36,000 Lives, Data Show." *The New York Times*, May 20, 2020, 1. https://www.nytimes.com/2020/05/20/us/coronavirus-distancing-deaths.html.

Godman, Heidi. "Have One Autoimmune Disease? You May Be at Risk for Another. U.s. News & World Report," January 26, 2018. https://health.usnews.com/health-care/patient-advice/articles/2018-01-26/have-one-autoimmune-disease-you-may-be-at-risk-for-another.

Godoy, Maria, and Daniel Wood. "What Do Coronavirus Racial Disparities Look Like State by State? NPR," May 30, 2020. https://www.npr.org/sections/health-shots/2020/05/30/865413079/what-do-coronavirus-racial-disparities-look-like-state-by-state.

Goldin, Ian. *Divided Nations: Why Global Governance Is Failing, and What We Can Do about It*. 1. ed. Oxford: Oxford Univ. Press, 2013.

Guardian Staff. "The Observer View on the Failure to Secure a Global Ceasefire During the Pandemic \Textbar Observer Editorial. The Guardian," May 24, 2020. http://www.theguardian.com/commentisfree/2020/may/24/the-observer-view-on-the-failure-to-secure-a-global-ceasefire-during-the-pandemic.

Gustin, Georgina. "The Paris Climate Problem: A Dangerous Lack of Urgency," November 7, 2019. https://insideclimatenews.org/news/07112019/paris-climate-agreement-pledges-lack-urgency-ipcc-timeline-warning.

Hamilton, Alexander, James Madison, John Jay, and Hamilton-Madison-Jay. *The Federalist Papers: Includes a Copy of the Constitution with Cross-References, Brief Précis of Each Essay, Index of Ideas, Copies of the Declaration of Independence and Articles of Confederation*. 1. Signet Classic pr. A Signet Classic. New York, NY: Signet Classic, 2003.

Hatcher, William S. "The Concept of Spirituality," 1982. https://www.bahai.org/documents/essays/hatcher-dr-william-s/concept-spirituality.

Henley, William Ernest. *Book of Verses.* 3d ed. New York: Scribner & Welford, 1891. https://www.google.com/books/edition/_/pxw1AAAAMAAJ?hl=en&pli=1&authuser=2.

Hibbs, Thomas. "Mandela: Long Walk to Freedom. National Review," December 21, 2013. https://www.nationalreview.com/2013/12/mandela-long-walk-freedom-thomas-hibbs/.

Hoopes, Townsend, and Douglas Brinkley. *FDR and the Creation of the u.n.* New Haven; London: Yale University Press, 1997.

Horowitz, Jason. "Italy's Right Links Low Birthrate to Fight Against Abortion and Migration (Published 2019)." *The New York Times*, March 27, 2019, 10. https://www.nytimes.com/2019/03/27/world/europe/italy-verona-salvini-world-congress-of-families.html.

Horsey, David. "Nelson Mandela Transformed Himself and Then His Nation. Los Angeles Times," December 6, 2013. https://www.latimes.com/opinion/topoftheticket/la-xpm-2013-dec-06-la-na-tt-nelson-mandela-20131206-story.html.

Hubbard, Ben. "As Smoke Clears in Beirut, Shock Turns to Anger." *The New York Times*, August 5, 2020, 1. https://www.nytimes.com/2020/08/05/world/middleeast/beirut-explosion-lebanon.html.

IAEA. "Additional Protocol. International Atomic Energy Agency," June 2016. https://www.iaea.org/topics/additional-protocol.

Ignatius, David. "Coronavirus Will Test Whether the Planet Can Unite in the Face of a Global Crisis. The Washington Post," February 25, 2020. https://www.washingtonpost.com/opinions/coronavirus-

will-test-whether-the-planet-can-unite-in-the-face-of-a-global-crisis/2020/02/25/
f44195c8-5818-11ea-9000-f3cffee23036_story.html.

Intergovernmental Panel on Climate Change. "Summary for Policymakers of IPCC Special Report on Global Warming of 1.5°c Approved by Governments. IPCC," October 8, 2018. https://www.ipcc.ch/2018/10/08/summary-for-policymakers-of-ipcc-special-report-on-global-warming-of-1-5c-approved-by-governments/.

Intergovernmental Science-Policy Platform on Biodiversity and Ecosystem Services. "Media Release: Nature's Dangerous Decline 'Unprecedented'; Species Extinction Rates 'Accelerating.' IPBES," May 7, 2019. https://ipbes.net/news/Media-Release-Global-Assessment.

International Commission on Intervention and State Sovereignty, Gareth J. Evans, Mohamed Sahnoun, and International Development Research Centre (Canada), eds. *The Responsibility to Protect: Report of the International Commission on Intervention and State Sovereignty*. Ottawa: International Development Research Centre, 2001.

Jabr, Ferris. "How Does a Caterpillar Turn into a Butterfly? Scientific American," August 20, 2012. https://www.scientificamerican.com/article/caterpillar-butterfly-metamorphosis-explainer/.

Jones, Sam. "The Fall of Rajoy: How gürtel Affair Defeated Spain's Great Survivor. The Guardian," June 1, 2018. https://www.theguardian.com/world/2018/jun/01/fall-of-mariano-rajoy-gurtel-spain.

Kann, Drew. "The Amazon Is a Key Buffer Against Climate Change. A New Study Warns Wildfires Could Decimate It. CNN," January 10, 2020. https://www.cnn.com/2020/01/10/world/amazon-rainforest-wildfires-climate-change-study/index.html.

Kelman, Steve, Ronald Sanders, Gayatri Pandit, and Sarah Taylor. "'Tell It Like It Is': Groupthink, Decisiveness, and Decision-Making Among u.s. Federal Subcabinet Executives." Harvard Kennedy School, August 2014. https://ash.harvard.edu/files/ kelman_sanders_pandit_taylor_tell_it_like_it_is.pdf.

Khurshudyan, Isabelle. "Wildfires Ravaged Siberia Last Year. This Spring, the Blazes Are Starting Even Bigger." May 16, 2020. https://www.washingtonpost.com/world/europe/ wildfires-ravaged-siberia-last-year-this-spring-the-blazes-are-starting-even-bigger/2020/05/15/ c00bdb50-9446-11ea-87a3-22d324235636_story.html.

Kingkade, Tyler. "US Police See Rise in Domestic Violence Calls Amid Coronavirus Lockdown. NBC News," April 5, 2020. https://www.nbcnews.com/news/us-news/police-see-rise-domestic-violence-calls-amid-coronavirus-lockdown-n1176151.

Kissinger, Henry A. "The Coronavirus Pandemic Will Forever Alter the World Order." *Wall Street Journal*, April 3, 2020. https://www.wsj.com/articles/the-coronavirus-pandemic-will-forever-alter-the-world-order-11585953005.

Kupferschmidt, Kai. "'A Completely New Culture of Doing Research.' Coronavirus Outbreak Changes How Scientists Communicate." *Science*, February 26, 2020. https://doi.org/ 10.1126/science.abb4761.

Lamy, Pascal. "Global Governance: Lessons from Europe." Invited address. Bocconi University: Invited address, November 9, 2009. https://www.wto.org/english/news_e/ sppl_e/sppl142_e.htm.

Landler, Mark, and Stephen Castle. "As Prime Minister, Boris Johnson Struggles to Find His Voice." *The New York Times*,

June 11, 2020, 24. https://www.nytimes.com/2020/06/10/
world/europe/britain-boris-johnson-racism.html.

Larson, Christina, and Matthew Brown. "Scientists Seek Rare
Species Survivors Amid Australia Flames. ABC News,"
January 18, 2020. https://abcnews.go.com/Technology/
wireStory/scientists-seek-rare-species-survivors-amid-
australia-flames-68366122.

Larson, Erik. "New Research: Diversity + Inclusion = Better
Decision Making at Work. Forbes," September 21, 2017.
https://www.forbes.com/sites/eriklarson/2017/09/21/new-
research-diversity-inclusion-better-decision-making-at-
work/.

Laya, Arancha González. "Opinion \Textbar as We Fight the
Pandemic, It's Clear the World Wasn't Ready. Here's How
to Fix That." March 25, 2020.
https://www.washingtonpost.com/opinions/2020/03/25/
we-fight-pandemic-its-clear-world-wasnt-ready-heres-how-
fix-that/.

Lee, Erika. *America for Americans: A History of Xenophobia in
the United States*. First edition. New York: Basic Books,
2019.

Levi, Michael A., and Michael E. O'Hanlon. *The Future of
Arms Control*. Washington, D.C: Brookings Institution
Press, 2005.

Loria, Kevin. "The World Health Organisation Is Worried
about Disease x and You Should Be Too. World Economic
Forum," March 15, 2018. https://www.weforum.org/
agenda/2018/03/a-mysterious-disease-x-could-be-the-next-
pandemic-to-kill-millions-of-people-heres-how-worried-
you-should-be/.

Ma'ani-Ewing, Sovaida. *Bridge to Global Governance: Tackling
Climate Change, Energy Distribution and Nuclear*

Proliferation. Center for Peace & Global Governance, 2018.

———. "We Owe It to Ourselves to Elect Honest and Trustworthy Leaders. Peace and Collective Security," March 7, 2020. http://collectivesecurity.blogspot.com/2020/03/we-owe-it-to-ourselves-to-elect-honest.html.

Mahbubani, Kishore. "The Boat Adrift. Outlook," 2010. https://www.outlookindia.com/website/story/the-boat-adrift/268197.

Matthew Lee, Gannon, Kathy, and Altman, Howard. "All US Troops to Leave Afghanistan in 14 Months If Taliban Meets Commitments of Peace Deal. Military Times," February 29, 2020. https://www.militarytimes.com/news/your-military/2020/02/29/all-us-troops-to-leave-afghanistan-in-14-months-if-taliban-meets-commitments-of-peace-deal-signed-today/.

Mazzetti, Mark, David E. Sanger, and William J. Broad. "U.s. Examines Whether Saudi Nuclear Program Could Lead to Bomb Effort." *The New York Times*, August 6, 2020, 1. https://www.nytimes.com/2020/08/05/us/politics/us-examines-saudi-nuclear-program.html.

McElvoy, Anne. *The Economist Asks: Jeffrey Sachs*, n.d. https://www.economist.com/podcasts/2020/06/11/will-covid-19-reverse-globalisation.

———. *Who Can Lead Britain Through Brexit?* Accessed October 12, 2020. https://www.economist.com/podcasts/2019/06/06/who-can-lead-britain-through-brexit.

Mecklin, John. "Current Time. Bulletin of the Atomic Scientist," January 23, 2020. https://thebulletin.org/doomsday-clock/current-time/.

Ministry for Europe {and} Foreign Affairs, France. "A Strong Europe in a World of Uncertainties. France Diplomatie," June 28, 2016. https://www.diplomatie.gouv.fr/en/french-foreign-policy/europe/news/article/a-strong-europe-in-a-world-of-uncertainties-28-06-16.

Myers, Steven Lee. "China's Voracious Appetite for Timber Stokes Fury in Russia and Beyond." *The New York Times*, April 9, 2019, 4. https://www.nytimes.com/2019/04/09/world/asia/chinas-voracious-appetite-for-timber-stokes-fury-in-russia-and-beyond.html.

NAACP. "Criminal Justice Fact Sheet. NAACP." Accessed October 9, 2020. https://www.naacp.org/criminal-justice-fact-sheet/.

Naím, Moisés. *The End of Power: From Boardrooms to Battlefields and Churches to States, Why Being in Charge Isn't What It Used to Be*. New York: Basic Books, A Member of the Perseus Books Group, 2013.

Norland, Erik. "Trade War Costs to Consumers, Companies and Nations. Financial Times Brandsuite." Marketing. Accessed October 12, 2020. https://www.ft.com/brandsuite/cme-group/trade-war-costs-consumers-companies-nations/index.html.

NYT Staff. "Suspect Is Charged with Arson in Oregon Wildfire. The New York Times," September 11, 2020. https://www.nytimes.com/2020/09/11/us/wildfires-live-updates.html.

Onishi, Norimitsu, and Selam Gebrekidan. "South Africa Vows to End Corruption. Are Its New Leaders Part of the Problem?" *The New York Times*, August 4, 2018, 1. https://www.nytimes.com/2018/08/04/world/africa/south-africa-anc-david-mabuza.html.

Peçanha, Sergio, Sarah Almukhtar, and K. K. Rebecca Lai. "Untangling the Overlapping Conflicts in the Syrian War. The New York Times," October 18, 2015. https://www.nytimes.com/interactive/2015/10/16/world/

middleeast/untangling-the-overlapping-conflicts-in-the-
syrian-war.html?searchResultPosition=1.

Pew Research Center. "Public's Mood Turns Grim; Trump
Trails Biden on Most Personal Traits, Major Issues." Pew
Research Center, June 30, 2020.
https://www.pewresearch.org/politics/2020/06/30/
publics-mood-turns-grim-trump-trails-biden-on-most-
personal-traits-major-issues/.

Pierre-Louis, Kendra. "The Amazon, Siberia, Indonesia: A
World of Fire (Published 2019)." *The New York Times*,
August 28, 2019, 1. https://www.nytimes.com/2019/08/
28/climate/fire-amazon-africa-siberia-worldwide.html.

Rácz, András. "African Comeback. Berlin Policy Journal,"
March 2020. https://berlinpolicyjournal.com/african-
comeback/.

Reuters Staff. "Beirut Port Blast Death Toll Rises to 190.
Reuters," August 30, 2020. https://www.reuters.com/
article/us-lebanon-crisis-blast-casualties-
idUSKBN25Q08H.

———. "Timeline: Key Dates in the u.s.-China Trade War.
Reuters," January 15, 2020. https://www.reuters.com/
article/us-usa-trade-china-timeline-idUSKBN1ZE1AA.

Rich, Nathaniel. "Losing Earth: The Decade We Almost
Stopped Climate Change. The New York Times Magazine,"
August 1, 2018. https://www.nytimes.com/interactive/
2018/08/01/magazine/climate-change-losing-earth.html.

Rio, Giulia McDonnell Nieto del. "Dry Thunderstorms Could
Accelerate the California Wildfires. The New York Times,"
August 23, 2020. https://www.nytimes.com/2020/08/23/
us/dry-thunderstorms-california-fires.html.

Ripple, William J., Christopher Wolf, Thomas M. Newsome,
Phoebe Barnard, and William R. Moomaw. "World

Scientists' Warning of a Climate Emergency." *BioScience* 70, no. 1 (January 2020): 8–12. https://doi.org/10.1093/biosci/biz088.

Rohn, E. James, and Chris Widener. *Twelve Pillars*. United States; Lake Dallas, Tex.: Jim Rohn International; Chris Widener International ; Distributed by www.YourSuccessStore.com, 2015.

Roosevelt, Franklin D., and Winston S. Churchill. "Declaration of Principles Issued by the President of the United States and the Prime Minister of the United Kingdom." North Atlantic Treaty Organization, August 14, 1941. http://www.nato.int/cps/en/natohq/official_texts_16912.htm.

Sanger, David E., and Lara Jakes. "Iran Is Accused of Hiding Suspected Nuclear Activity." *The New York Times*, June 19, 2020, 9. https://www.nytimes.com/2020/06/19/us/politics/iran-nuclear-iaea.html.

Sanger, David E., Eric Lipton, Eileen Sullivan, and Michael Crowley. "Before Virus Outbreak, a Cascade of Warnings Went Unheeded." *The New York Times*, March 21, 2020, 1. https://www.nytimes.com/2020/03/19/us/politics/trump-coronavirus-outbreak.html.

Sang-Hun, Choe. "Park Geun-Hye, Ex-South Korean Leader, Gets 25 Years in Prison (Published 2018). The New York Times," August 24, 2018. https://www.nytimes.com/2018/08/24/world/asia/park-geun-hye-sentenced-south-korea.html.

Santora, Marc. "Poland Bashes Immigrants, but Quietly Takes Christian Ones (Published 2019)." *The New York Times*, March 26, 2019, 4. https://www.nytimes.com/2019/03/26/world/europe/immigration-poland-ukraine-christian.html.

Schell, Jonathan. *The Seventh Decade: The New Shape of*

Nuclear Danger. New York; Godalming: Holt ; Melia [distributor], 2008.

Schmidt, Charles. "Coronavirus Researchers Tried to Warn Us. Undark," June 8, 2020. https://undark.org/2020/06/08/for-experts-who-study-coronaviruses-a-grim-vindication/.

SciTechDaily Staff. "Scientists Warned China Was a 'Time Bomb' for Novel Coronavirus Outbreak in 2007. SciTechDaily," March 22, 2020. https://scitechdaily.com/scientists-warned-that-china-was-a-time-bomb-for-novel-coronavirus-outbreak-in-2007/amp/.

Scripps Research Institute. "Up to 45 Percent of SARS-CoV-2 Infections May Be Asymptomatic. Science Daily," June 12, 2020. https://www.sciencedaily.com/releases/2020/06/200612172208.htm.

Shoghi Effendi. *Call to the Nations: Extracts from the Writings of Shoghi Effendi*. [Haifa, Israel] : Wilmette, Ill: Bahá'í World Centre ; Distributed in the U.S. by Bahá'í Publishing Trust, 1977.

Singh, Prerna. "Nationalism Can Have Its Good Points. Really. The Washington Post: Monkey Cage," January 26, 2018. https://www.washingtonpost.com/news/monkey-cage/wp/2018/01/26/nationalism-can-have-its-good-points-really/.

Smith, David. "New York's Andrew Cuomo Decries 'eBay'-Style Bidding War for Ventilators. The Guardian," March 31, 2020. https://www.theguardian.com/us-news/2020/mar/31/new-york-andrew-cuomo-coronavirus-ventilators.

Snyder, Timothy. *On Tyranny: Twenty Lessons from the Twentieth Century*. First edition. New York: Tim Duggan Books, 2017.

Staff, AFP. "The Mighty Nile, Threatened by Waste, Warming, Mega-Dam. France 24," March 20, 2020. https://www.france24.com/en/20200320-the-mighty-nile-threatened-by-waste-warming-mega-dam.

Stevis-Gridneff, Matina. "A €750 Billion Virus Recovery Plan Thrusts Europe into a New Frontier." *The New York Times*, May 27, 2020, 1. https://www.nytimes.com/2020/05/27/world/europe/coronavirus-europe-bailout.html.

Stockholm International Peace Research Institute. "Global Military Expenditure Sees Largest Annual Increase in a Decade—Says SIPRI—Reaching $1917 Billion in 2019. SIPRI," April 27, 2020. https://www.sipri.org/media/press-release/2020/global-military-expenditure-sees-largest-annual-increase-decade-says-sipri-reaching-1917-billion.

Stopping Lockdown Domestic Abuse on My Street, 2020. https://www.bbc.com/news/av/world-53014211.

Symonds, Alexandria. "Amazon Rainforest Fires: Here's What's Really Happening." *The New York Times*, August 23, 2019, 1. https://www.nytimes.com/2019/08/23/world/americas/amazon-fire-brazil-bolsonaro.html.

Taylor, Jim. "Personal Growth: How to Align Your Values and Your Life. The Power of Prime," May 14, 2012. http://www.psychologytoday.com/blog/the-power-prime/201205/personal-growth-how-align-your-values-and-your-life.

Telegraph Foreign Staff. "Death of the Nile: Egypt Fears Ethiopian Dam Will Cut into Its Water Supply. The Telegraph," October 2, 2017. https://www.telegraph.co.uk/news/2017/10/02/death-nile-egypt-fearsethiopian-dam-will-cut-water-supply/.

The International Crisis Group. "The Responsibility to Protect: When It's Right to Fight. The International Crisis Group," July 2003. https://www.crisisgroup.org/global/responsibility-protect-when-its-right-fight.

Titley, David. "Why Is Climate Change's 2 Degrees Celsius of

Warming Limit so Important?" August 22, 2017.
http://theconversation.com/why-is-climate-
changes-2-degrees-celsius-of-warming-limit-so-
important-82058.

Toynbee, Arnold Joseph. *Change and Habit: Challenge of Our Time*. Reprinted. Global Thinkers Social Issues / Environment. Oxford: Oneworld [u.a.], 1992.

Turkewitz, Julie. "The Amazon Is on Fire. So Is Central Africa." *The New York Times*, August 27, 2019, 7. https://www.nytimes.com/2019/08/27/world/africa/congo-angola-rainforest-fires.html.

United Nations, ed. *In Larger Freedom: Towards Development, Security and Human Rights for All: Report of the Secretary-General*. New York: United Nations, Dept. of Public Information, 2005.

———. "The Recovery from the COVID-19 Crisis Must Lead to a Different Economy. United Nations." Accessed October 10, 2020. https://www.un.org/en/un-coronavirus-communications-team/launch-report-socio-economic-impacts-covid-19.

United Nations FCCC Conference of the Parties. "Paris Agreement, Conference of the Parties, Report No. 21, Addendum." In *COP Report No. 21*, Treaty Collection:XXVII.7.d. Treaties. Paris, France: United Nations, 2015. https://treaties.un.org/doc/Treaties/2016/02/20160215.

United Nations General Assembly. "Resolution Adopted by the General Assembly on 16 September 2005," October 24, 2005. https://www.un.org/en/development/desa/population/migration/generalassembly/docs/globalcompact/A_RES_60_1.pdf.

United Nations High Commissioner for Refugees. "Figures at a

Glance. UNHCR the Refugee Agency," June 18, 2020. https://www.unhcr.org/figures-at-a-glance.html.

United Nations News Staff. "Greta Thunberg Tells World Leaders 'You Are Failing Us,' as Nations Announce Fresh Climate Action. UN News," September 23, 2019. https://news.un.org/en/story/2019/09/1047052.

Universal House of Justice. Letter. "18 January 2019 – to the Bahá'ís of the World." Letter, January 18, 2019. https://www.bahai.org/library/authoritative-texts/the-universal-house-of-justice/messages/20190118_001/1#821441849.

———. Letter. "October 1985 - to the Peoples of the World." Letter, October 1985. https://www.bahai.org/library/authoritative-texts/the-universal-house-of-justice/messages/19851001_001/19851001_001.pdf.

Urban Institute. "Structural Racism in America," April 2020. https://www.urban.org/features/structural-racism-america.

Washington, George. "Farewell Address - Saturday, September 17, 1796," September 19, 1796. https://founders.archives.gov/documents/Washington/99-01-02-00963.

Washington Post Staff. "Full Text: Donald Trump Announces a Presidential Bid. Washington Post," June 16, 2015. https://www.washingtonpost.com/news/post-politics/wp/2015/06/16/full-text-donald-trump-announces-a-presidential-bid/.

Welz, Adam. "Fire Fallout: How Ash and Debris Are Choking Australia's Rivers. Yale Environment 360," February 27, 2020. https://e360.yale.edu/features/fire-fallout-how-ash-and-debris-are-choking-australias-rivers.

Willsher, Kim. "François Fillon Found Guilty of Embezzling Public Funds," June 29, 2020.

http://www.theguardian.com/world/2020/jun/29/
francois-fillon-found-guilty-of-embezzling-public-funds.

WION Web Team. "Curfew Imposed in 40 Cities Including
Washington DC as Protests Spread Across US. World Is
One (WION)," June 1, 2020. https://www.wionews.com/
world/curfew-imposed-in-40-cities-including-washington-
dc-as-protests-spread-across-us-302235.

'Abdu'l-Bahá. *Selections from the Writings of 'abdu'l-Bahá*. 1st
U.S. pocket-size ed. Wilmette, Ill: Bahá'í Pub. Trust, 1997.

'Abdu'l-Bahá, Marzieh Gail, and Ali-Kuli Khan. *The Secret of
Divine Civilization*. 1st Bahá'í Pub. ed. Wilmette, Ill: Bahá'í
Pub. Trust, 2007. https://www.bahai.org/library/
authoritative-texts/abdul-baha/secret-divine-civilization/.

Index

220

Sovaida Ma'ani Ewing writes and lectures in the area of global governance, peace, and international security. Prior to her current work as founding director of the Center for Peace and Global Governance, Ms. Ma'ani Ewing served as an Attorney-Advisor in the Legal Advisor's Office of the U.S. State Department. Born in East Africa and raised there and in the Middle East, she has also lived in the United Kingdom, where she earned an LLM in International Law and European Union Law at Cambridge University and qualified as a barrister-at-law of England and Wales. She subsequently moved to the United States and qualified as an attorney-at-law there, practiced law at respected law firms in Washington, D.C., including her own, and taught as an adjunct professor of law at George Washington University's law school. Ms. Ma'ani Ewing has written several books including four in her area of work, listed below. She maintains a blog about principled solutions to current global issues at
http://collectivesecurity.blogspot.com

Also by Sovaida Ma'ani Ewing:

Collective Security within Reach

Building a World Federation: The Key to Resolving Our Global Crises

21st Century Ready: How You Can Help Solve the Global Problems of Our Times

Bridge to Global Governance: Tackling Climate Change, Energy Distribution and Nuclear Proliferation

Printed in the USA
CPSIA information can be obtained
at www.ICGtesting.com
LVHW050732060324
773704LV00001B/101

9 781733 157810